S0-ARY-603

FAITH UNTAMED

THE STRENGTH OF RAHAB, DEBORAH, AND ABIGAIL

IVEY HARRINGTON BECKMAN

Faith Untamed: The Strength of Rahab, Deborah, and Abigail
© 2008 Serendipity House

Published by Serendipity House Publishers
Nashville, Tennessee

All rights reserved. No part of this work may be reproduced, stored in a retrieval system, or transmitted in any form or by any means, electronic or mechanical, including photocopying and recording, without express written permission of the publisher. Requests for permission should be addressed to Serendipity House, One LifeWay Plaza, Nashville, TN 37234-0175.

ISBN: 978-1-5749-4422-8
Item 005126277
Dewey Decimal Classification: 248.843
Subject Headings:
FAITH \ WOMEN \ CHRISTIAN LIFE

Scripture quotations marked HCSB® are taken from the *Holman Christian Standard Bible®*, copyright © 1999, 2000, 2002, 2003 by Holman Bible Publishers. Used by permission.

Scriptures marked The Message are taken from *THE MESSAGE®*. Copyright © 1993, 1994, 1995, 1996, 2000, 2001, 2002. Used by permission of NavPress Publishing Group.

Scriptures marked NIV are taken from the *Holy Bible, New International Version*, copyright © 1973, 1978, 1984 by International Bible Society.

Scriptures marked NASB are taken from the *New American Standard Bible®*, Copyright © 1960, 1962, 1963, 1968, 1971, 1972, 1973, 1975, 1977, 1995 by the Lockman Foundation. Used by permission. (www.lockman.org)

To purchase additional copies of this resource or other studies:
ORDER ONLINE at *www.SerendipityHouse.com*;
WRITE Serendipity House, 117 10th Avenue North, Nashville, TN 37234
FAX (615) 277-8181 ~ PHONE (800) 525-9563

1-800-525-9563
www.SerendipityHouse.com

Printed in the United States of America

CONTENTS

Faith Untamed

HOME...WORKS
MARRIAGE & FAMILY SERIES

Check these and other great studies at www.SerendipityHouse.com ...

Some Assembly Required: Instructions for an Amazing Marriage

Dream Team: The Power of Two

Turning Up the Heat: Rekindle Romance and Passion

Coauthoring Your Child's Story: Parenting on Purpose

Can You Hear Me Now?: Communication in Marriage

Creating Mutual Funds: Financial Teamwork in Marriage

Faith Untamed

Faith Untamed

THE STRENGTH OF RAHAB, DEBORAH, JAEL & ABIGAIL

"NEVER UNDERESTIMATE THE POWER OF A WOMAN."

Long before *Ladies Homes Journal* introduced "the power of a woman" into our vernacular, four unconventional ladies lived this wisdom with extraordinary strength and character. They generated the sort of unbridled power that propelled them from who they were to whom God designed them to become.

Rahab, Deborah, Jael, and Abigail were an incredible mix. Forces of nature and nurture, they embraced their femininity without compromising the strength inherent in their being. They replaced cultural norms—often establishing a new standards—with faith in action because they were God-motivated and God-gifted to accomplish great things. And while fear may have caused them to tremble at times, these ladies didn't bat an eye when it came to getting their hands dirty.

It's important to note that along their courageous paths, these four women didn't dislike men, go out of their way to compete against men, or seek to one-up them. Instead, they worked in close and respectful partnership with them. Their anthem was not "I am woman, hear me roar!" but "I'm a woman, use me, Lord!"

In *Faith Untamed* you'll get to know four heroic women unapologetic about upsetting the status quo and more than willing to let loose the power of God through their own circumstances:

* Rahab – A prostitute with a hero's heart
* Deborah – A forward-thinking woman who wasn't afraid of a fight
* Jael – A real camper who packed a wallop
* Abigail – A multi-tasking beauty with brains

The Women of Purpose series highlights ordinary women used by God in extraordinary ways. As we delve below the surface and into the hearts of these women, we discover not only who they are, but also who we are. We find our hearts awakening to deeper intimacy with God and to an increasing desire to give ourselves to something grand, noble, and bigger than ourselves. We don't have to settle for simply existing; God created us to really live—to be women of passion and women of purpose.

AGAINST THE WALL

RAHAB

If asked which female Bible character they'd first want to speak with in heaven, few people would respond, "Rahab." The biography of this engaging prostitute is usually overshadowed by more dignified dames. But don't sweat the slight; the women of Jericho, Rahab's hometown, shunned her, too. Rahab lived a carnal life in the company of men with money in their pockets and one thing on their minds. Was she beautiful? We're not told. But we do know she was a fighter. A strike force of female wit and will.

By the time we meet her in the Book of Joshua, Rahab had arrived at a pivotal moment in her life. By choice or circumstance, Rahab was physically, socially, and financially cornered by the walls of Jericho. But when her back was against the wall and she was forced to make a life-threatening choice, she put her trust in the one true God. This lady of the night, who certainly knew how to make a grand entrance, proved she also knew when and how to make a grand exit. Drawing from the strength within, she recognized God's voice deep within her tarnished soul even when the dissonance of her culture was at full volume. That soft, still voice gave her the faith and courage to do what was right when it mattered most.

God weaves into every woman abilities and personality traits ripe for His use. Even better, His grace accepts no boundaries. God is continually willing to use less than perfect women — those easily tagged "unsuitable" — to accomplish His holy purpose with style. Forget prim and proper. Rahab is about to rattle any misperceptions about the proper etiquette and background needed to become an ancestor — or even a follower — of Christ.

BREAKING THE ICE   *10-15 Minutes*

LEADER INSTRUCTIONS FOR THE GROUP EXPERIENCE:
These "Breaking the Ice" experiences are designed to get people talking and keep things moving. They help group members get acquainted with one another. Encourage participants to introduce themselves by completing the sentence. Explain that answers can refer to something physical, relational, emotional, spiritual, or humorous.

1. Introduce yourself and then complete this sentence: "Because I'm a woman, people sometimes underestimate my ability to ..."

LEADER: For this session, bring a DVD of the movie The Sandlot. Before the session begins, cue the DVD to scene 12: "A Challenge." (Show 44:00-46:45). See the notes on p. 90 for additional instructions.

These naive boys are guilty of underestimating the power of the "weaker sex." In their minds, "You play like a girl!" is the ultimate insult, the gauntlet for all-out war. This ultimate insult, however, is only indicative of their extreme naiveté.

2. What female characters or personalities in our culture do you most admire? Why? Describe their strengths.

Even in our seemingly progressive culture, women are often stereotyped as inferior in sports and even in intellectual arenas. For instance, the first time diminutive Connie Rhea stepped up to bat at her church's mixed softball game, all the men in the outfield moved closer infield. Connie knew what they were thinking: "Small girl. Easy out." But what they didn't know would cost them. Connie was a gifted athlete. Connie chose a bat that was a bit heavier than what a woman would typically use, gripped it high, intentionally swung just a hair late—and powered the ball over the heads of the stunned right fielders. The next time Connie was up to bat, the outfielders backed up. They learned a valuable lesson.

3. How do the typical feminine stereotypes make you feel?

God doesn't see us through a stereotypical lens. He sees personalities, strengths, weaknesses, and abilities that we often fail to recognize in our perceptions of self and others. Rahab's story proves that God finds strength in the unconventional and unexpected.

DISCOVERING THE TRUTH
20-25 Minutes

LEADER: In "Discovering the Truth," ask various group members to read the Bible passages aloud. Be sure to leave time for the "Embracing the Truth" and "Connecting" segments that follow this discussion. Show chapter 22, "Benny's Dream" from The Sandlot. *(Show 1:14:17 to 1:17:39).* *See p. 90 for additional instructions.*

PUTTING SURVIVAL SKILLS TO WORK

Joshua son of Nun secretly sent two men as spies from Acacia Grove, saying, "Go and scout the land, especially Jericho." So they left, and they came to the house of a woman, a prostitute named Rahab, and stayed there.

JOSHUA 2:1, HCSB

The city of Jericho was the gateway to the heart of the promised land, the Middle Eastern acreage God promised to Abraham's descendants. Rahab's house was located on the wall of the city. (Some scholars believe her home was actually built into the wall.) Contrary to our modern-day Wall Street, Jericho's Wall Street was in the low-rent district of the city. From her vantage point she probably had a view not only of the city itself but also of the area outside the protective walls. This view may have given her an advantage in running her business.[1]

LEADER: Discuss as many discovery questions as time permits. Encourage participation by inviting different individuals to respond. It will help to highlight in advance the questions you don't want to miss. Be familiar with the "Scripture Notes" at the end of this session.

1. Do you think the two spies purposely chose Rahab's house because of its Wall Street location, or did she go out of her way to wave them in? Explain.

2. Do you think Rahab's use of her gifts and skills was acceptable to God? Explain. If not, then why do you think He chose her as a part of this mission?

Session One

3. Assuming there were other women in Jericho, what do you think it could have been about Rahab that made her appealing for God's plan?

4. What do you think Rahab's role in the fall of Jericho says about the attributes God requires in some situations?

Rahab's name actually means *"fierce"* or *"tenacious."* She certainly needed moxie to run a shady and dangerous business in the culture of her day. In those days a female didn't own a corner of Jericho real estate unless she had street smarts. But we're about to see redemption totally turn Rahab's life around. Isn't it just like God to gift a woman with life skills and to redeem them for His purposes even after a series of missteps?

5. At a glance Rahab wouldn't seem to be the sort of woman we've come to expect God to use. Using what you know, write in the first column those traits that initially seem to be too "untamed." In the second indicate how God could redeem these qualities and use them to accomplish His purposes.

Personality trait   How God could use it for His glory

_____   _____

_____   _____

_____   _____

Principle for Living
Let people feel the weight of who you are. No one — regardless of her career or choices — is beyond God's redemptive power.

RATTED OUT AND COVERED UP

It didn't take long for someone to rat out the spies harbored under Rahab's care. So much for "what happens on the wall stays on the wall." The tale of Rahab's alliance with the Israelites is about to become more intense.

²The king of Jericho was told, "Look, some of the Israelite men have come here tonight to investigate the land." ³Then the king of Jericho sent word to Rahab and said, "Bring out the men who came to you and entered your house, for they came to investigate the entire land." ⁴But the woman had taken the two men and hidden them.

JOSHUA 2:2-4a, HCSB

LEADER: As a group, brainstorm possible "rat" candidates. Who blew the whistle on Rahab's guests? List possibilities and vote for the "Most Likely Rat."

We're not told how long the spies stayed with Rahab before they were ratted out, but one thing is clear: Rahab chose their agenda over that of her own people.

6. What factors do you think may have led Rahab to ally herself with foreign spies and the God of the Israelites?

At its root, saving faith involves an act of trust in what is known. Rahab's awareness of God's protection of the Israelites may have been enough to ignite her faith. (See Joshua 2:8-11.) Rahab's trust in God was in infancy, but she had boundless enthusiasm to act on it even under intense pressure.

7. Why do you think Rahab, whose faith in God was so new, was willing to risk her life to ally with the Israelites?

⁴[Rahab] said, "Yes, the men did come to me, but I didn't know where they were from. ⁵At nightfall, when the gate was about to close, the men went out, and I don't know where they were going. Chase after them quickly, and you can catch up with them!" ⁶But she had taken them up to the roof and hidden them among the stalks of flax that she had arranged on the roof. ⁷The men pursued them along the road to the fords of the Jordan, and as soon as they left to pursue them, the gate was shut.

JOSHUA 2:4B-7, HCSB

Session One

How much time Rahab had to plan we do not know, but the custom of the day prohibited a man from barging into a woman's house (even a prostitute's) without her permission. At the very least, she had minutes to decide whether or not to protect the Israelite spies as well as figuring out where and how best to hide them.

8. In what ways do you think cunning could be used for something other than deceit?

Interestingly enough, the men at the door didn't balk at Rahab's explanation of where the strangers had gone. Perhaps she was known as a woman of her word. Had she been caught in this twisting of the facts, Rahab and her entire family would have faced terrible consequences.

WE'VE GOT TO TALK

⁸Before the [spies] fell asleep, she went up on the roof ⁹and said to them, "I know that the LORD has given you this land and that dread of you has fallen on us, and everyone who lives in the land is panicking because of you. ¹⁰For we have heard how the LORD dried up the waters of the Red Sea before you when you came out of Egypt, and what you did to Sihon and Og, the two Amorite kings you completely destroyed across the Jordan. ¹¹When we heard this, we lost heart, and everyone's courage failed because of you, for the LORD your God is God in heaven above and on earth below."

JOSHUA 2:8-11, HCSB

Rahab's belief and her willingness to come to the defense of strangers illustrates faith in action. But it wasn't blind faith. Rahab trusted the history of the Israelite people and rested her future in the hands of the God who parted seas and decimated armies for them.

9. How do you think Rahab's personality or "wiring" might have contributed to her willingness to follow the God of Israel?

By trusting God and the two spies sent into Jericho, Rahab expressed a willingness to leave her old life behind. While her ethics in lying to cover for the spies may seem weak, we must remember that her faith was likely new and her knowledge of God limited. But in spite of any weaknesses or character flaws Rahab may have had, we must concede that her steely resolve is to be admired! She trusted God enough to ally herself with Him, even though doing so might have cost her life.

Principle for Living

When you reach a pivotal life point, remember what God has done. Trust Him to take care of your future and act on your faith in Him.

EMBRACING THE TRUTH
15-20 Minutes

LEADER: *This section focuses on helping group members integrate what they've learned from the Bible into their own hearts and lives. Invite volunteers to read the Bible passages aloud.*

Rahab's is a story of courage in the face of danger. While God equipped her with the wit and quick thinking to overcome, some of us may feel less ready for adventure. Maybe we struggle with having courage. Perhaps we balk at the idea of telling others about our faith or fear embarrassment over a perceived shortcoming. But we can know that God does not require us to go through life alone. He helps us through life's challenges. He gives us the strength to overcome our weaknesses, and yes, even the bravery to let ourselves be dramatically used for His purposes—even when it seems frightening to do so. Scripture is clear that God is our very present help in times of danger.

*²⁹He gives strength to the weary
    and increases the power of the weak.
³⁰Even youths grow tired and weary,
    and young men stumble and fall;
³¹but those who hope in the LORD
    will renew their strength.
They will soar on wings like eagles;
    they will run and not grow weary,
    they will walk and not be faint.*

ISAIAH 40:29-31, NIV

Rahab was a woman who sensed that there was something more for her. She was unwilling to believe the voices that reinforced the lie: "This is all you'll ever be good for."

LEADER: Ask participants to share examples of times when their faith pushed them through fear and to action.

1. What is the greatest obstacle you've ever overcome? How did a personal strength, like a personality trait, help you?

2. How can we be "weak" and "strong" at the same time? Explain how this paradox was evident in Rahab's story.

3. Describe a time when you felt God strengthening you in the midst of your weakness. What did you learn about God through that experience? About yourself?

4. Consider Rahab's emotions as she harbored the spies and covered for them. How do you think her perception of God's strength and sovereignty was impacted by her experience?

Session One

Because of her faith in what she had heard of Him, God blessed Rahab's efforts and protected her from certain death. God honors faith. When we have faith in Him, He will do great things in and through our lives, too.

Principle for Living
God can use your personal strengths and even weaknesses for His glory. Have faith in Him; He will see you through.

CONNECTING
10-15 Minutes

THE LIES YOU BELIEVE

LEADER: Use "Connecting" as a time to begin to bond with, encourage, and support one another. Invite everyone to join in the discussions. Ask participants to gather into pairs, each reading aloud the dialogue of either Edward or Vivian.

In the movie *Pretty Woman*, Edward (played by Richard Gere) asks Vivian (played by Julia Roberts) how someone like her became a prostitute. Their discussion follows:

Vivian: People put you down enough, you start to believe it.
Edward: I think you are a very bright, very special woman.
Vivian: The bad stuff is easier to believe. You ever notice that?

LEADER: Provide small pieces of paper and felt-tip pens. While the women are in pairs, ask them to write down the "bad stuff" they believe about themselves that causes them to underestimate their potential. After allowing time to reflect and write, ask each pair to put these in a fireplace, garbage can, or some other means of disposal.

Rahab's story reminds us that life isn't always neat and clean, with perfect corners. In fact, life can be quite the opposite. But in the messes where we often find ourselves, there is one sure thing: although sin's signature remains, those who have chosen Jesus are new creations.

LEADER: Help participants replace the lies they've believed about themselves with the truth. On colorful note cards, create a set of the following verses for each woman. Use a different color for each verse. Encourage participants to place the verses in the suggested places and recite them aloud each day, inserting their name in the blanks. These passages of Scripture will help them soak in the truths, helping them to see their potential through God's eyes.

On Your Bathroom Mirror:

"Good morning, _____!
You're beautiful with God's beauty,
Beautiful inside and out."
> Luke 1:28, The Message

On Your Dashboard:

"Listen, _____, *'consider and give ear:*
Forget your people and your father's house.
The king is enthralled by your beauty;
honor him, for he is your lord.'"
> Psalm 45:10-112, NIV

On your Refrigerator:

"For you created _____'s *inmost being;*
you knit me together in my mother's womb.
I praise you because I am fearfully and wonderfully made;
your works are wonderful,
I know that full well."
> Psalm 139:13-14, NIV

On Your Computer:

"_____ *can do everything through him who gives me strength.*"
> Philippians 4:13, NIV

LEADER: Take some time to go over the "Group Covenant" at the back of this book (page 101). Now is the time for each person to pass around her book to collect contact information in the Group Directory on page 104.

Session One

Share and record group prayer requests that you will regularly pray over between now and the next session. In addition to doing this, pray together that God will strengthen and encourage each participant as she takes her heart's deepest questions to God this week.

PRAYER REQUESTS:

TAKING IT HOME

LEADER: Explain that the "Taking It Home" sections contain introspective questions as well as offering questions to take to God. Encourage each person to set aside quiet time this week so she can make the most of this study and group experience. Be sure to highlight the importance of writing down thoughts, feelings, and key insights that God reveals. Journaling is a powerful tool.

Studying God's truth is not an end in itself. Our goal is always heart and life change. To take the next step of integrating truth into our lives, we need to (1) look honestly into our hearts to understand the true motivations that drive us and (2) seek God's perspective on our lives. Psalm 51:6 says God "desire[s] truth in the innermost being" (NASB)

A Question to Take to My Heart

The following question asks you to look into your heart and focus on your deepest feelings about yourself. Our behaviors are the best indicators of what we really believe. Look deep into the underlying beliefs down in your heart where your truest attitudes and motivations live. Spend some time reflecting, and don't settle for a quick answer.

What is the greatest obstacle that stands between the woman I am today and the woman God designed me to be?

A Question to Take to God

When you ask God a question, expect His Spirit to guide your heart to discover His truth. Be careful not to rush or manufacture an answer. Don't write down what you think the "right answer" is. Don't turn the Bible into a spiritual reference book or encyclopedia. Just pose a question to God and wait on Him. Remember, the litmus test for anything we hear from God is alignment with the Bible as our ultimate truth source. Keep a journal of the insights you gain from your time with God.

God, how do you feel about the obstacles in my life?

SCRIPTURE NOTES

JOSHUA 2:1-11

2:1-24 The theme of this story is risk. Rahab, the prostitute, risked her own life by harboring Joshua's spies. The spies themselves took great risk by trusting Rahab's instructions and her vow of silence. As a result of their combined risks, Joshua received the go-ahead from the spies' report and prepared to conquer the city of Jericho.

2:1 Acacia Grove. This probably identifies the most striking physical feature of the town. Acacia wood is hard-grained and repels insects. The ark of the covenant and the wooden portions of the tabernacle were made of acacia wood (Ex. 36:20; 37:1). *came to the house of … a prostitute.* City prostitutes in the ancient world often ran inns. This simplified procurement of clients. The spies were seeking no more than lodging in a public house where information could be overheard.

2:2 The king of Jericho. Many cities of the ancient Near East were independent city-states with hereditary monarchs. (See the list of city-state kings in Genesis 14:1-2 and Joshua 12:9-24.)

2:4 So she said. Rahab lied to the king's men. There are three primary views about lying to protect someone. (1) In extreme circumstances, a lie is acceptable behavior. (2) A lie is always wrong, but sometimes it is a lesser wrong than the consequences of telling the truth. (3) A lie is always wrong. An alternative to lying must be found. In Rahab's case, it's hard to imagine avoiding a lie without giving away the spies. Yet, we must avoid the temptation to let the ends justify the means.

2:6 she had taken them up. The flax she was drying on her flat roof made a perfect hiding spot for her fugitives. *stalks of flax.* Flax is the source of the fibers from which linen is made. Flax stalks were soaked in water to separate the fibers from the stems. The fibers were pulled apart and spread on flat rooftops to dry in the sun before being woven into linen.

2:8-11 the LORD your God is God. Rahab put a strange amount of faith in two people she hardly knew. And why was she so convinced of their God? After all, she was a prostitute, not a parishioner. Even so, Rahab heard about the wonders the Lord performed for Israel and believed in Him. Her fellow countrymen quaked in dread, but they did not turn to God in faith. Consequently, Rahab is honored in the New Testament as a woman of great faith (Heb. 11:31) and became a part of Jesus' lineage (Matt. 1:5).

ISAIAH 40:29-31

40:31 trust in the LORD. Implies confident
expectation rather than passive
resignation (see Ps. 40:1). Faith brings
spiritual transformation. Weary captives
returning from the exile would be
emotionally uplifted.

PSALM 45:10-12

45:10-11 he is your lord. The royal bride is
a foreigner. She must forget her people
and be loyal to the king. Though the
details of this marriage are not revealed,
royal marriages were often political
alliances.

PSALM 139:13-14

139:13 You who created. God is the One
who creates the unique mental and
physical attributes of each individual.
This implies loving care for each detail
of our own complexity.

SESSION QUOTATIONS

1 Ann Spangler and Jean S. Syswerda,
   Women of the Bible, (Grand Rapids,
   MI: Zondervan Publishing House,
   1999), p. 103.

SIMPLY RED

RAHAB MAKES A DEAL

In our last session Rahab sent the bounty hunters off in the wrong direction, confident they'd be gone long enough to allow time for Rahab to make a deal. After taking a deep breath, she was ready to make a deal with the undercover agents hiding beneath her flax. In doing so, Rahab confronted a stack of issues ranging from "Who do I believe myself to be?" to "What can I do to help my family?" Not the least of her concerns was surely wondering whether Isreal's God would accept her. Would He choose to overlook what she'd done and actually protect her among His own?

Rahab's is a story of courage and redemption. It's a story about a passionate and noble heart. She sacrificed the familiar in order to gain access to the One True God who was likely very foreign to her at the time. Out of Rahab's willingness to align herself with the Lord came unprecedented personal freedom, a clean start, and the honor due a hero of the faith.

BREAKING THE ICE - *15-20 Minutes*

LEADER INSTRUCTIONS FOR THE GROUP EXPERIENCE: These icebreakers are intended to help get group members talking. To get women speculating about Rahab's life, divide them into two teams. Ask Group A to consider factors that may have necessitated Rahab's choice to become a prostitute. Encourage Group B to consider what kind of life circumstances might have forced Rahab into the lifestyle. After a few minutes of discussion, ask a spokesperson from each group to share their group's thoughts.

Group A: What personal convictions or motivations do you think may have prompted Rahab to *choose* a life of prostitution?

Group B: What situations or circumstances do you think may have *forced* Rahab into a life of prostitution?

Groups A and B: Do you think the manner in which Rahab became a prostitute—whether by force or choice—changes her value in God's eyes? Why or why not?

LEADER: Encourage participants to share key insights from last session's "Taking It Home" questions. This should only take a couple of minutes, but allow a little extra time if needed. Affirm those who spent quiet time with God this week.

DISCOVERING THE TRUTH

20-25 Minutes

LEADER: In "Discovering the Truth," ask various group members to read the Bible passages aloud. Be sure to leave time for the "Embracing the Truth" and "Connecting" segments that follow.

NEGOTIATIONS

Regardless of the reason behind her profession, Rahab didn't waste the spies' time by making excuses for the path her life traveled. It seems she had a "what's done is done" attitude toward it. Perhaps her apparent silence on the issue was based on hope. Her encounter with two of God's favored ones, Israel's spies, gave her hope that her life could change for the better.

12"Now please swear to me by the LORD that you will also show kindness to my family, because I showed kindness to you. Give me a sure sign 13that you will spare the lives of my father, mother, brothers, sisters, and all who belong to them, and save us from death."

14The men answered her, "We will give our lives for yours. If you don't report our mission, we will show kindness and faithfulness to you when the LORD gives us the land."

JOSHUA 2:12-14, HCSB

LEADER: Discuss as many discovery questions as time permits. Encourage participation by inviting different individuals to respond. It will help to highlight in advance the questions you don't want to miss. Be familiar with the "Scripture Notes" at the end of this session.

1. Why do you think Rahab asked the spies to guarantee her family's safety? What could this say about her sense or loyalty, her backstory, or even her family relationships?

2. What in Rahab's words in verses 12 and 13 show her "growing trust in the Lord?"

3. In making this deal with the soon-to-be invaders, Rahab would lose … (Check all that apply.)
   ❐ the allegiance of her countrymen
   ❐ any possible safety her Jericho citizenship may have offered
   ❐ her self-respect
   ❐ her source of income
   ❐ her family
   ❐ God's love

4. Why is it important that a person be willing to sacrifice in order to pursue God?

Principle for Living
Pride, security, relationships, cash. We have to step out in faith in order to step into the adventure God has in store. This often requires leaving behind everything that's familiar.

ROPE TRICKS

¹⁵ Then [Rahab] let [the spies] down by a rope through the window, since she lived in a house that was built into the wall of the city. ¹⁶"Go to the hill country so that the men pursuing you won't find you," she said to them. "Hide yourselves there for three days until they return; afterwards, go on your way."

¹⁷ The men said to her, "We will be free from this oath you made us swear, ¹⁸unless, when we enter the land, you tie this scarlet cord to the window through which you let us down. Bring your father, mother, brothers, and all your father's family into your house. ¹⁹If anyone goes out the doors of your house, his blood will be on his own head, and we will be innocent. But if anyone with you in the house should be harmed, his blood will be on our heads. ²⁰And if you report our mission, we are free from the oath you made us swear."

²¹"Let it be as you say," she replied, and she sent them away. After they had gone, she tied the scarlet cord to the window.

JOSHUA 2:15-21, HCSB

Likely Rahab had helped a few wayward husbands out the window of her home because the rope needed appears to have been close by. The back wall of Rahab's home was most likely the first-tier fortification wall around the city of Jericho. Scholars have estimated the height of this mud brick wall to be between 20 to 26 feet high.[1]

5. How do you think Rahab's choice of occupation contributed to her ability to get this job done? What does this say about breadth and depth of God's redemption?

6. What sort of internal dialogue do you think raged in Rahab's heart as she tied the cord? In what ways can you relate to that dialogue?

Session Two

THE WAITING GAME

The two spies hit the ground running. They had lots to tell their leader, Joshua. But first they had to hide for a few days to be sure they weren't followed.

²²So the two men went into the hill country and stayed there three days until the pursuers had returned. They searched all along the way, but did not find them.

JOSHUA 2:22, HCSB

Rest assured, our fierce and determined Rahab wasn't sitting on her laurels while the spies were biding their time. She was herding her relatives like cattle. Prodding. Poking. Perhaps like getting your family out the door in the morning times fifty!

7. Why do you think God would allow anyone in Jericho, including Rahab, to escape when *"the city and everything in it [were] set apart to the LORD for destruction" (Joshua 6:17)*?

Session Two

EVENTS UNFOLD

²³Then the [spies] returned, came down from the hill country, and crossed the Jordan. They went to Joshua son of Nun and reported everything that had happened to them. ²⁴They told Joshua, "The LORD has handed over the entire land to us. Everyone who lives in the land is also panicking because of us."

JOSHUA 2:23-24, HCSB

¹²Joshua got up early the next morning. The priests took the ark of the LORD, ¹³and the seven priests carrying seven trumpets marched in front of the ark of the LORD. While the trumpets were blowing, the armed troops went in front of them, and the rear guard went behind the ark of the LORD. ¹⁴On the second day they marched around [Jericho] once and returned to the camp. They did this for six days.

JOSHUA 6:12-14, HCSB

Imagine yourself in Rahab's situation as the "enemy" with whom she'd allied began daily marching the outer perimeter of her city. Soldiers marched around Jericho once a day for six days but nothing else happened. Surely from her scarlet-draped window she could witness people sitting on the walls laughing and jeering at the soldiers below, perhaps even throwing things on them. It's possible that her family may have considered her mad at some points, pestering her with questions such as, "Why isn't anything happening?" and "Can't we just go outside for a bit? It's crowded in here."

8. Given what you know, do you think Rahab was patient during this time? Why or why not?

Principle for Living

Trusting God can be difficult. You must remember to cling to Him in times of trial. Just as He promised to hand Jericho over to His people, He has promised never to leave or forsake you. Believe Him!

RAHAB AND HER FAMILY SPARED

[15]Early on the seventh day, [the Israelite army] started at dawn and marched around the city seven times in the same way. That was the only day they marched around the city seven times. [16]After the seventh time, the priests blew the trumpets, and Joshua said to the people, "Shout! For the LORD has given you the city. [17]But the city and everything in it are set apart to the LORD for destruction. Only Rahab the prostitute and everyone with her in the house will live, because she hid the men we sent."

[20]So the people shouted, and the trumpets sounded. When they heard the blast of the trumpet, the people gave a great shout, and the wall collapsed. The people advanced into the city, each man straight ahead, and they captured the city. [21]They completely destroyed everything in the city with the sword—every man and woman, both young and old, and every ox, sheep, and donkey.

JOSHUA 6:15-17,20-21, HCSB

9. In being "right," how do you think Rahab felt as she watched the destruction? Do you think she felt vindicated? Do you think she experienced a sense of loss, or do you think it was more of a time for celebrating a new future?

10. Describe a time when you have huddled on your own wall like Rahab—refusing to submit to doubt before seeing God's power become evident around you.

²²Joshua said to the two men who had scouted the land, "Go to the prostitute's house and bring the woman out of there, and all who are with her, just as you promised her." ²³So the young men who had scouted went in and brought out Rahab and her father, mother, brothers, and all who belonged to her. They brought out her whole family and settled them outside the camp of Israel.

²⁴They burned up the city and everything in it, but they put the silver and gold and the articles of bronze and iron into the treasury of the LORD's house. ²⁵But Joshua spared Rahab the prostitute, her father's household, and all who belonged to her, because she hid the men Joshua had sent to spy on Jericho, and she lives in Israel to this day.

JOSHUA 6:22-25, HCSB

In Hebrews 11, a "hall of faith" is recorded; it's essentially a record of believers who placed their faith in God and thus found honor in His eyes. Verse 31 states: *"By faith Rahab the prostitute received the spies in peace and didn't perish with those who disobeyed"* (HCSB). This short passage proves that you don't have to be perfect—far from it, in fact— for God to use you in amazing ways. It was Rahab's choice rather than her past that saved her entire family and gained her honor for all time.

LEADER: Have the group read aloud this customized version of Hebrews 12:1.

Therefore since we also have such a large cloud of witnesses surrounding us, let us [as strong women of God] lay aside every weight and the sin that so easily ensnares us, and run with endurance the race that lies before us.

HEBREWS 12:1, HCSB

Rahab's story "shows us that God's grace accepts no boundaries. The red cord that saved Rahab and her family reminds us of the red blood of Jesus Christ, who still saves us today, and of Isaiah's words, *'though your sins may be as scarlet, they shall be as white as snow.'* Rahab put her faith in the God of Israel and was not disappointed."[2] As a result of her willingness to align herself with God in spite of her personal shortcomings, Rahab found a place of honor as a true hero of faith.

Principle for Living
In order to experience all that God has for you, you must make a personal choice to join Jesus in His mission and embrace your new life in Him. This will require stepping out of your comfort zone and your complacency

---

THE SPY WHO LOVED HER

[1]The historical record of Jesus Christ, the Son of David, the Son of Abraham:
[2]Abraham fathered Isaac,
Isaac fathered Jacob,
Jacob fathered Judah and his brothers,
[5]Salmon fathered Boaz by Rahab,
Boaz fathered Obed by Ruth,
Obed fathered Jesse,
[6]and Jesse fathered King David.

MATTHEW 1:1-2,5-6, HCSB

11. How does having Rahab in the lineage of Jesus comment on the women God uses? What does this say about God's heart?

A look at Rahab's story is incomplete without a look at the love story that followed her bold faith decision. Salmon, one of the two spies she had hidden, saw beyond Rahab's past and gave her a future with him. He asked her to become his wife, and she accepted. Remarkably, Scripture tells us that Rahab was the mother of Boaz and thus in the bloodline of Christ Himself. Rahab, the prostitute turned faith heroine, was the great, great, great ... great-grandmother of Jesus!

Five women, none of them perfect, are listed among the ancestors of Christ. It's highly unusual for women to be named in Hebrew genealogies at all. Yet Matthew 1 mentions five women, and all of them are notable, and at least three were disgraced by their own sin.

Principle for Living

God is not only able but also willing to repay what has been lost. He grieves some of the choices we make, but He is always ready to meet us where we are and put our stories to work for His purposes.

EMBRACING THE TRUTH

15-20 Minutes

LEADER: This section focuses on helping group members integrate what they've learned from the Bible into their own hearts and lives. Invite volunteers to read the Bible passages aloud.

CAN YOU SEE ME NOW?

1. Describe a time when someone saw you for what you could be rather than what you were. How did that make you feel?

2. Why do you think God opened His heart to all peoples and not just the Jews? How does knowing He counts you among His own make you feel about yourself?

Briefly explain how the following Scriptures serve as adoption papers to those who choose to accept Christ.

¹⁶The Spirit Himself testifies together with our spirit that we are God's children, ¹⁷and if children, also heirs — heirs of God and co-heirs with Christ — seeing that we suffer with Him so that we may also be glorified with Him.

ROMANS 8:16-17, HCSB

¹The Spirit of the Sovereign Lord is on me,
because the Lord has anointed me
to preach the good news to the poor.
He has sent me to bind up the brokenhearted,
to proclaim freedom for the captives
and release from darkness for the prisoners,
²to proclaim the year of the LORD's favor
and the day of vengeance of our God,
to comfort all who mourn,
³and provide for those who grieve Zion —
to bestow on them a crown of beauty
instead of ashes,
the oil of gladness
instead of mourning,
and a garment of praise
instead of a spirit of despair.
They will be called oaks of righteousness,
a planting of the LORD
for the display of his splendor.

ISAIAH 61:1-3, NIV

Rahab was adopted into the family of God by faith. We, too, are among His adopted children when we become Christ followers.

Session Two

Principle for Living

If you've placed faith in Christ and asked Him to be Lord of your life,
you — like Rahab — are a child of God.

CONNECTING - *10-15 Minutes*

LEADER: Use "Connecting" as a time to begin to bond with and support one another. Invite everyone to join in the discussions. For this week's "Connecting," visit a fabric store and purchase strands of red cording or ribbon. Gift each woman with two cords. Encourage them to use one as a bookmark to remind them of the vital importance of living by faith every day. Ask participants to think of a family member who does not know Christ and to hold the second cord in honor of that person during today's prayer. Ask them to silently pray with you as you say aloud:

"Father, I praise you for the wonderful and unexpected ways you have acted in my life. Let the knowledge of your faithfulness increase my courage to take the risks that faith demands.

Leader: Encourage everyone to give their second scarlet cord to a lost family member and to share the Rahab's story with them.

Share and record group prayer requests that you will regularly pray over between now and the next session. In addition to doing this, pray together that God will strengthen and encourage each participant as she takes her heart's deepest questions to God this week.

PRAYER REQUESTS

TAKING IT HOME

LEADER: Again, there are a couple of questions to focus on this week in "Taking It Home." Encourage each participant to set aside quiet time this week so she can make the most of this study and group experience. Be sure to highlight the importance of writing down thoughts, feelings, and key insights that God reveals.

A QUESTION TO TAKE TO MY HEART

The following question asks you to look into your heart and focus on your deepest feelings about yourself. Our behaviors are the best indicators of what we really believe deep down. Look deep into the underlying beliefs down in your heart where your truest attitudes and motivations live. Spend some time reflecting, and don't settle for a quick answer.

❧ What about my life stands in most need of God's power of redemption?

A QUESTION TO TAKE TO GOD

When you ask God a question, expect His Spirit to guide your heart to discover His truth. Be careful not to rush or manufacture an answer. Don't write down what you think the "right answer" is. Don't turn the Bible into a spiritual reference book or encyclopedia. Just pose a question to God and wait on Him. Remember, the litmus test for anything we hear from God is alignment with the Bible as our ultimate truth source. Keep a journal of the insights you gain from your time with God.

❧ God, when did you grieve with me while I was unaware?

Session Two

Scripture Notes

JOSHUA 2:12-24

2:1-24 The theme of this story is risk. Rahab, the prostitute, risked her own life by harboring Joshua's spies. And the spies themselves took great risk by trusting Rahab's instructions and her vow of silence. As a result of their combined risk, Joshua received the go-ahead from the spies' report and prepared to conquer the city of Jericho.

2:12 Give me a sure sign. Realizing she had spared their lives, Rahab took the opportunity to negotiate a tremendous favor from the two spies. Perhaps strengthened by her own confession, she wanted their assurance that the physical and also spiritual health of her family would be protected.

2:14 our lives for yours. A serious transaction had taken place and bonded three total strangers. Rahab rescued them from certain death. Rahab herself would soon barely escape the destruction of her city.

2:15 built into the wall of the city. Rahab likely made her home—an original high-rise apartment—on planks supported between the two walls surrounding the city of Jericho.

2:16 the hill country. Rahab sent the spies deeper into Canaan. Jericho lay below sea level in the Jordan Valley. The hills west of Jericho soared more than 3,000 feet above sea level and offered countless hiding places within their rugged heights.

The king's soldiers meanwhile had hurried east to guard the fords of the Jordan (v. 7).

2:18 scarlet cord. To distinguish Rahab's house from the other houses in Jericho, the Israelites would look for a dyed cord dangling from her window. Rahab eagerly hung the cord, a symbol of her faith, as soon as the men left. The scarlet color of the cord hung upon her window as a symbol of her salvation and a sign that all in her house were to be protected is reminiscent of the Passover in Egypt (Ex. 11–12) and another preview of Jesus' blood shed for our salvation.

2:19 his blood will be on his own head. The spies took responsibility for the chance of a mistake. If anyone in Rahab's family were harmed during the attack, the spies would take the blame. However, if a member of the family left the safety of Rahab's house, the Israelites could not be held responsible.

2:22 into the hill country … three days. Hiding spots by the dozens awaited the spies as they traveled toward this cave-ridden area of Palestine. Since they were reported to have left through the city gate, the king's men looked for them along the road to the Jordan River.

JOSHUA 6:12-17,20-24

6:17 set apart to the LORD for destruction. To be "set apart," when God was speaking of cities under His personal judgment, meant that these were to be completely destroyed. Much like a burnt offering, the entire city of Jericho was to be set aside as a sacrifice.

HEBREWS 12:1

12:1 witnesses. This is the same word used for "martyrs." It is probably a deliberate play on words in which both meanings are intended. The heroes of faith are pictured as a cheering section of former runners in a race urging the contemporary readers to persevere as they did. *lay aside every weight.* In Greek games at the time, runners ran with no clothes so that they could move freely without hindrance. *the sin that so easily ensnares.* Just as a flowing robe makes it impossible to run well, so sin makes the Christian life difficult.

ISAIAH 61:1-3

61:1 to proclaim liberty. Jesus read these verses from a scroll in the synagogue (see Luke 4:16-21). All who heard knew these verses to be a prophecy of the Messiah. Jesus said that He was fulfilling them.

61:3 a crown of beauty. In place of the ashes that signify mourning, the Israelites will wear a crown symbolizing joy (Ps. 30:11). This is to be a time of celebration—the mourning period is over.

SESSION QUOTATIONS

1 Bryant Wood, "The Walls of Jericho," *Answers Magazine* [online], March 1999 [accessed February 14, 2008]. Available from the Internet: *www.answersingenesis.org.*

2 Ann Spangler and Jean E. Syswerda, *Women of the Bible: A One Year Devotional Study of Women in Scripture* (Grand Rapids, MI: Zondervan, 1999), 102.

Session Two

BUSINESS—NOT AS USUAL

DEBORAH

Two hundred years after the walls of Jericho fell and Rahab began a new life among God's family, Israel continued in the fight for the promised land. The idolatry the Canaanites practiced was like a cancer running rampant in the land. Under the oppression and fierce opposition they faced, the people of God were in constant peril.

In those dark days, God's people were led not by a coalition of men but by the wisdom of judges. These judges functioned in roles that ranged from arbitrator to military general to president to spiritual leader. The Book of Judges focuses on several of these wise heroes of the faith, but one of the most intriguing periods of this era in the history of Israel chronicles an event during the leadership of Deborah. During a tense relationship with Canaan, the fate of the Israel nation hinged on her leadership.

BREAKING THE ICE - *10-15 Minutes*

LEADER INSTRUCTIONS FOR THE GROUP EXPERIENCE: These "Breaking the Ice" experiences will relax participants. Make this time fun. For this session, bring a DVD of the movie Star Wars. Before the session begins, cue the DVD to chapter 26, "Alderaan's Fate.". (Show from 57:00 to 59:10.) You may also use an additional clip: chapter 32, "Rescuing the Princess" (1:14:11 to 1:19:04). After watching the scene, discuss the following question as a group:

1. If you watched the premiere of the first movie in the *Star Wars* saga, try to remember whether you were impressed by Princess Leia or turned off by her strong personality. How does your recollection of your first impression of Princess Leia differ from your perception today? Explain.

Session Three

2. Some of the men Princess Leia encountered treated her like a damsel in distress. Others assumed that she was out of her element. What do you think Princess Leia knew about herself that others didn't?

3. Brainstorm a list of fictional or historical female characters who assumed important roles in war and diplomacy. What qualities, if any, do those characters share?

LEADER: Encourage participants to share a key insight from last session's "Taking it Home." This should only take a couple of minutes, but allow a little more time if it's needed.

DISCOVERING THE TRUTH
20-25 Minutes

LEADER: In "Discovering the Truth," ask various group members to read the Bible passages aloud. Be sure to leave time for the "Embracing the Truth" and "Connecting" segments that follow this discussion.

WHAT'S A WOMAN LIKE YOU DOING IN A PLACE LIKE THIS?

By the time Deborah appeared on history's scene, the national anthem for the Israelites could have been, "Here We Go Again." The people repeated the same weary cycle of rebellion against God, facing His retribution, crying out to Him in repentance, and seeking His gracious restoration time and time again.

After many years of this, the Israelites found themselves under the brutality of Jabin, King of Hazor. Sisera, captain of the king's army, and his 900 ironclad chariots rolled over the Israelite people, flattening their pride, crushing their courage, and seriously denting their faith in God. No man in Israel would challenge Sisera and his heavy metal, but one unlikely heroine was willing to step into the vacuum of leadership left behind.

¹The Israelites again did what was evil in the sight of the LORD after Ehud had died. ²So the LORD sold them into the hand of Jabin king of Canaan, who reigned in Hazor. The commander of his forces was Sisera who lived in Harosheth of the Nations. ³Then the Israelites cried out to the LORD, because Jabin had 900 iron chariots, and he harshly oppressed them 20 years.

⁴Deborah, a woman who was a prophet and the wife of Lappidoth, was judging Israel at that time. ⁵It was her custom to sit under the palm tree of Deborah between Ramah and Bethel in the hill country of Ephraim, and the Israelites went up to her for judgment.

JUDGES 4:1-5, HCSB

1. How many different roles do you think Deborah managed in the course of a day? What does this reveal to you about her strengths?

Deborah, whose name means "honeybee," appears to have been a homemaker at the time she was selected for service to her country. In Scripture her personal identity is defined simply as "prophet" and "the wife of Lappidoth." There is no aristocratic lineage or educational resume attached to her name, but Deborah's story suggests that she was totally in touch with who she was—well aware of her strengths

2. How do you think Deborah became the judge of Israel? What personal attributes do you think may have led to this role for Deborah?

3. What do you think God saw in Deborah that would lead Him to establish her in this role?

No doubt while Deborah was sitting in judgment under that palm tree there were some terse "you are only a woman" reminders and a few "who does she think she is?" snipes. It appears, however, that over the years of turmoil—when the normal way of doing things was no longer possible because the civil court system was inept and the military too weak to defend its national borders—Deborah had proven her counseling skills worthy and her relationship with God strong.

4. How do you think Deborah could have used her role as judge to build unity and confidence among the Israelites?

5. How do you think Deborah's faith contributed to an ability to draw from her strength yet compensate for her weaknesses?

Principle for Living

God can use your personal strengths, as well as your role in the home and/or business place, to build unity and point others to Him. Welcome Him to use you for His purposes.

SMART MOVES

Israel's female judge seemed always ready to accept God's call into adventure. As complete annihilation at the hands of Sisera's forces became inevitable, Deborah found herself in a unique position to influence Israel's response to his advance.

⁶[Deborah] summoned Barak son of Abinoam from Kedesh in Naphtali and said to him, "Hasn't the LORD, the God of Israel, commanded you: 'Go, deploy the troops on Mount Tabor, and take with you 10,000 men from the Naphtalites and Zebulunites? ⁷Then I will lure Sisera commander of Jabin's forces, his chariots, and his army at the Wadi Kishon to fight against you, and I will hand him over to you.'"

⁸Barak said to her, "If you will go with me, I will go. But if you will not go with me, I will not go."

⁹"I will go with you," she said, "but you will receive no honor on the road you are about to take, because the LORD will sell Sisera into a woman's hand." So Deborah got up and went with Barak to Kedesh. ¹⁰Barak summoned Zebulun and Naphtali to Kedesh; 10,000 men followed him, and Deborah also went with him.

JUDGES 4:6-10, HCSB

6. Look again at Judges 4:9 above. Do you think this is a rebuke? If so, do you think Deborah could have responded to Barak's request, or condition, better? How would you have responded to Barak?

7. Why do you think Barak wanted Deborah to go into battle with him?

Principle for Living
A true leader takes action when necessary but also inspires others to do so. Ask God to help you use your strengths to help others accept His invitation into the story He is revealing.

SERVICE AS A LIFESTYLE

¹I commend to you our sister Phoebe, who is a servant of the church which is at Cenchrea; ²that you receive her in the Lord in a manner worthy of the saints, and that you help her in whatever matter she may have need of you; for she herself has also been a helper of many, and of myself as well.

ROMANS 16:1-2

In Romans 16:1 Paul used the Greek word *diakonos* to describe Phoebe's ministry in the church. This word, translated "servant," can also refer to the role of deacon within the church. While Phoebe likely served in some official capacity within the church at Cenchrea, clearly *diakonos* or servanthood was far more than a role for Phoebe—she had positive effects on everyone around her. Paul didn't highly praise Phoebe because of her servant role in the church, but rather because helping and serving others was a lifestyle![1]

8. How do you think Deborah's presence was also "far more than a role"? How do you think she came to understand her giftedness in these areas?

9. In what ways do you think Phoebe and Deborah were alike? Different?

Principle for Living
In our "me-first" world, servant hearts are powerful tools for transformation. Whatever you lovingly do to serve within your church will strengthen the body of believers and attract others through your active love to Jesus.

NOT AFRAID OF A FIGHT

¹²It was reported to Sisera that Barak son of Abinoam had gone up Mount Tabor. ¹³Sisera summoned all his 900 iron chariots and all the people who were with him from Harosheth of the Nations to the Wadi Kishon. ¹⁴Then Deborah said to Barak, "Move on, for this is the day the LORD has handed Sisera over to you. Hasn't the LORD gone before you?" So Barak came down from Mount Tabor with 10,000 men following him.

¹⁵The LORD threw Sisera, all his charioteers, and all his army into confusion with the sword before Barak. Sisera left his chariot and fled on foot. ¹⁶Barak pursued the chariots and the army as far as Harosheth of the Nations, and the whole army of Sisera fell by the sword; not a single man was left.

JUDGES 4:12-16, HCSB

When it was time to do battle, tremendous odds were against the Israelite army. They were vastly outnumbered and their weapons were inferior to the iron weaponry of the Canaanites. "Until David's time, the Israelites lacked knowledge of iron technology; thus their enemies like the Philistines, who had mastered ironworking, dominated them. Yet in response to a word from God, Deborah called out to the Israelites to do battle. She was held in such high respect that the reluctant Israelites complied, and 10,000 men assembled to confront the enemy."² The beheld 10,000 arrogant men and 900 ironclad chariots. But the dauntless spirit of Deborah didn't budge; she had God as her Ally.

10. Given her understanding of her role, why do you think Deborah chose not to command the army but let Barak lead the troops to battle?

Regardless of who was leading the Israelite offensive, Judges 5:4-5 reveals there was more than a little Divine Intervention on the battlefield that day.

⁴"O LORD, when you went out from Seir,
  when you marched from the land of Edom,
the earth shook, the heavens poured,
  the clouds poured down water.
⁵The mountains quaked before the LORD, the One of Sinai,
  before the LORD, the God of Israel."

JUDGES 5:4-5, HCSB

11. What do you think about the way God supports those who live boldly in their relationship with Him?

Principle for Living

God not only champions victims of injustice, but He also fights alongside those who valiantly step into the battles into which they are called.

EMBRACING THE TRUTH

15-20 Minutes

LEADER: *This section focuses on helping group members integrate what they've learned from the Bible into their own hearts and lives. Invite volunteers to read the Bible passages.*

1. Deborah calls herself the "mother of Israel" (Judges 5:7). What maternal attributes did Deborah exhibit, and how did these qualities translate into her "business"?

2. Take a few moments to discuss the doubts you think Deborah may have confronted. In what ways can you relate to Deborah? How could Deborah inspire you?

3. Has someone ever said, "You have a strong personality," giving you the distinct feeling it wasn't meant as a compliment? What adjustments might you need to make to ensure you are using your strengths for God's glory and not your own?

Choose one of the following verses from The Message as your personal battle hymn. Make it your goal to memorize it this week.

So if you find life difficult because you're doing what God said, take it in stride. Trust him. He knows what he's doing, and he'll keep on doing it.

1 PETER 4:19, HCSB

[13]If with heart and soul you're doing good, do you think you can be stopped? [14]Even if you suffer for it, you're still better off. Don't give the opposition a second thought. [15]Through thick and thin, keep your hearts at attention, in adoration before Christ, your Master.

1 PETER 3:13-15, HCSB

"I [God] see what you've done. Now see what I've done. I've opened a door before you that no one can slam shut. You don't have much strength, I know that; you used what you had to keep my Word. You didn't deny me when times were rough."

REVELATION 3:8, HCSB

CONNECTING - *10-15 Minutes*

LEADER: Use "Connecting" as a time to continue encouraging and supporting one another as you examine the thoughts, motives, and attitudes of your hearts. Invite everyone to join in the discussions.

1. The details about Deborah's husband and their marriage are absent from this story. What kind of man do you think Lappidoth was? Why?

2. How do you think Lappidoth supported Deborah?

3. Given the many hats she wore, how do you think Deborah
supported Lappidoth?

4. How do you use the strength God gifted you with to help those
around you?

TAKING IT HOME

LEADER: The "Taking it Home" sections contain introspective questions as well as offering questions to take to God. Encourage each person to set aside quiet time this week so she can make the most of this study and group experience. Be sure to highlight the importance of writing down thoughts, feelings, and key insights that God reveals.

Studying God's truth is not an end in itself. Our goal is always heart and life change. To take the next step of integrating truth into our lives, we need to (1) look honestly into our hearts to understand the true motivations that drive us, and (2) seek God's perspective on our lives. Psalm 51:6 says God "desire[s] truth in the innermost being" (NASB).

QUESTION TO TAKE TO MY HEART

The following question asks you to look into your heart and focus on your deepest feelings about yourself. Our behaviors are the best indicators of what we really believe deep down. Look deep into the underlying beliefs down in your heart where your truest attitudes and motivations live. Spend some time reflecting, and don't settle for a quick answer.

❧ *Which of my roles make me come alive?*

A QUESTION TO TAKE TO GOD

When you ask God a question, expect His Spirit to guide your heart to discover His truth. Be careful not to rush or manufacture an answer. Don't write down what you think the "right answer" is. Don't turn the Bible into a spiritual reference book or encyclopedia. Just pose a question to God and wait on Him. Remember, the litmus test for anything we hear from God is alignment with the Bible as our ultimate truth source. Keep a journal of the insights you gain from your time with God.

❧
God, how do I use my strengths in ways that bring a smile to Your face?

Scripture Notes

JUDGES 4:1-5, 6-10; 12-16

4:1-24 Once again, the Lord demonstrates His presence among the people in the form of a deliverer. Deborah, the judge at this time, directs a victorious military invasion under Barak against a Canaanite army.

4:1-2 Sisera. The Canaanite king ordered Sisera, his commander, to lead his troops in battle against Israel.

4:4 Deborah. Deborah reigned as a judge, settling disputes among the Israelites. As a spiritual leader or prophetess, she also predicted the victory for Israel's battle against the Canaanites and encouraged them to fight.

4:6 Barak. He was Deborah's top pick for commanding 10,000 troops to war against the enemy. His timidity led him to refuse to take leadership, so the glory of the battle went instead to a woman (v. 9).

4:7 I will lure Sisera. What seemed an ideal battleground for Sisera would soon turn to a muddy pit of disaster, according to the Lord's plan.

4:9 a woman's hand. Courage was up for grabs in this situation. Barak passed on the opportunity, and Deborah predicted that a woman would respond to God's call to courage and help secure the victory (vv. 18-22).

PSALM 20:7

20:7-8 Some take pride in a chariot. Chariots and horses were among the strongest and most effective tools in a good army, but they were subject to God's plans.

SESSION QUOTATIONS

[1] Women's Study Bible, page 389. Thomas Nelson. Dorothy Kelley Patterson and Rhonda Kelley, eds., *The Woman's Study Bible* (Nashville: Thomas Nelson, 1995), 389.

[2] Sue and Larry Richards, *Women of the Bible: The Life and Times of Every Women in the Bible* (Nashville: Thomas Nelson, 2003), 43.

MORE TO THE POINT

JAEL

In our last session Sisera managed to escape the massacre God planned for the Canaanite army. Likely enraged by the unflattering turn of events, he knew Barak couldn't be far behind him. The retreating general Sisera was far from safe. But where could he hide?

Ironically, the man so recently upstaged by a woman and her God was about to run headlong into a similar situation. This one, however, would prove inescapable. Sisera chose to claim sanctuary in the home of an acquaintance, blindly trusting that man's wife with his life and comfort. Unfortunately for Sisera, the mistake would prove his last. For Israel, however, the army leader's mishap would become an incredible—though unlikely—victory at the hands of yet another female warrior of the Lord. Jael would singlehandedly wipe out Israel's greatest foe.

BREAKING THE ICE - *10-15 Minutes*

LEADER INSTRUCTIONS FOR THE GROUP EXPERIENCE: These "Breaking the Ice" experiences are designed to jumpstart conversation and camaraderie. Play a recording of Karen Carpenter's song "Rainy Days and Mondays" to set the tone.

1. Judges 5:4 reveals that God thwarted Sisera and his army with a torrent of rain. Share a funny story about a time when a little rain caused a lot of trouble.

2. How can something as simple as rain remind us of how God works?

LEADER: Encourage participants to share key insights from last session's "Taking it Home" questions. This should only take a couple of minutes, but allow a little more time if someone has something inspiring to share. Affirm those who spent time seeking God about how they can better use their abilities for His glory.

3. As you searched your heart about areas where you should be leading or supporting, what did you learn about yourself? About God's plans for you?

DISCOVERING THE TRUTH

20-25 Minutes

LEADER: Invite various group members to read the Bible passages aloud throughout this section. Your group should be gelling well now, and good discussions should emerge. Encourage this, but watch your time. Be sure to leave time for the "Embracing the Truth" discussions and "Connecting" segment.

THE STAGE IS SET

¹⁵*At Barak's advance, the L*ORD *routed Sisera and all his chariots and army by the sword, and Sisera abandoned his chariot and fled on foot.* ¹⁶*But Barak pursued the chariots and army as far as Harosheth Haggoyim. All the troops of Sisera fell by the sword; not a man was left.*

¹⁷*Sisera, however, fled on foot to the tent of Jael, the wife of Heber the Kenite, because there were friendly relations between Jabin king of Hazor and the clan of Heber the Kenite.*

JUDGES 4:15-17, NIV

47

LEADER: Ask for a volunteer to read the following narrative aloud.

General Sisera stopped to catch his breath, knowing the stitch in his side was nothing compared to the agony of gutted pride he felt after such a humiliating slaughter. He kicked the ground in frustration—just before remembering that he'd lost his sandal in the muddy muck that had replaced his battlefield. Immediately blood oozed from his big toe, mingling with the filth caked between his others. He sat down hard on a jutting piece of rock, cursing the pain, Barak, Deborah, and the confounding rain that still fell in blowing sheets. *How can I be drenched to the bone and yet be thirsty?* he wondered.

Sisera quietly mulled over his options as lightning flashed across the desert sky. Where to go? Who to trust? "Heber the Kenite lives near here," he finally decided aloud, "I'll find sanctuary in his tents."

Using his last bit of strength, Sisera stood and quickened his pace in the direction of Heber's home and business. When he crested the next ridge, the rain suddenly stopped. To his relief, Sisera could see Jael, Heber's wife, standing outside her tent. Almost as if she had been waiting for him, Jael flashed a quick smile and waved. *She recognizes me as one of her husband's clients*, he thought to himself proudly as he made his way down the slippery hill.

Sisera entered into the sanctuary of Heber's property and Jael's hospitality, sagging with relief and drained with exhaustion.

LEADER: Discuss as many discovery questions as time permits. Encourage participation by inviting different individuals to respond. It will help to highlight in advance the questions you don't want to miss. Be familiar with the "Scripture Notes" at the end of this session.

1. In the story, Sisera seems relieved to see a familiar face. Are familiar faces always safe? Explain.

2. What immediate advantage did Jael have over the approaching Sisera?

THE PLOT THICKENS

Now Heber the Kenite had moved away from the Kenites, the sons of Hobab, Moses' father-in-law, and pitched his tent beside the oak tree of Zaanannim, which was near Kedesh.

JUDGES 4:11, HCSB

Of all the women listed among our featured heroines of untamed faith, Jael is certainly the wildest. "Jael" means "wild mountain goat," and the meaning certainly seems to ring true in the case of this valiant woman.

3. What can you conclude about Jael and Heber as a result of their decision to move away from family? Rahab found herself in a similar position with regards to her family. How do you think these decisions and situations might be associated with a faith untamed?

In Jael's day everything connected with tent keeping was a woman's job, and women became expert in all the phases of making, pitching, and striking tents. No doubt Jael's hands were strong, her arms muscular, and her aim true. She could hit a nail on the head every time. She also could lift and tote with the best of men, but she undoubtedly worked long and hard to get the job done.

When Jael and her husband moved closer to the military operations that might make use of Heber's metal working skills, Jael pitched their tents on Oak Tree Lane in the Zaanannim community, located close to the valley where God hosed Sisera and his army. We don't know if Jael saw the storm clouds in the distance or if she had been holed up inside her tent going stir crazy because of the rain. What we do know is that at some point she saw Sisera coming and could easily tell that he had a bad day on the battlefield. Perhaps seizing an opportunity she had long desired, Jael went out to meet the man she recognized by name and rank.

18Jael went out to greet Sisera and said to him, "Come in, my lord. Come in with me. Don't be afraid." So he went into her tent, and she covered him with a rug. 19He said to her, "Please give me a little water to drink for I am thirsty." She opened a container of milk, gave him a drink, and covered him again. 20Then he said to her, "Stand at the entrance to the tent. If a man comes and asks you, 'Is there a man here?' say, 'No.'"

JUDGES 4:18-20, HCSB

4. Compare and contrast Rahab's involvement with the spies with Jael's treatment of Sisera. Talk about their motivations.

5. Why do you think Sisera believed Jael would lie for him if a man came looking for him?

Apparently Heber's tribe was regarded as neutral to both the Canaanites and Israelites. Heber's people were descendants of Jethro, Moses' father-in-law, and hence had the confidence of the Israelites. Though they had suffered somewhat at the hands of the Canaanites, the tribe had made a formal contract of peace with King Jabin. In other words the Heber stand was "we don't have a dog in this fight."

So what was Jael's obligation after she invited the soaking wet, mud-caked, bone-tired general into her tent? According to the *International Standard Bible Encyclopedia*, "It is important to note that Sisera went into Jael's tent, not the tent of Heber, her husband. The ancient laws of hospitality in the Middle East were very strict. A guest, once *ritually* invited into the home, had to be protected and cared for, even at the expense of every one else in the home. But only the chief man of the household could offer ritual hospitality. Jael offered simple *help* to a fleeing army general, but not ritual [all encompassing] hospitality. [1] Bottom line? Jael wasn't obligated to protect Sisera.

DRIVING HOME HER POINT

While he was sleeping from exhaustion, Heber's wife Jael took a tent peg, grabbed a hammer, and went silently to Sisera. She hammered the peg into his temple and drove it into the ground, and he died.

JUDGES 4:21, HCSB

Sisera was a man on the run an anti-Israel general who had barely escaped with his life. It appears Jael had the situation pegged from the moment she saw Sisera approach her tent. Faced with a man far superior to her in physical strength, she used her wits and familiar tools to accomplish the unthinkable. Jael had one chance to hit the proverbial nail on the head, and she pinned Sisera's head to the ground. Of all the men who have ever underestimated the power of a woman, Sisera is the historical poster boy.

6. Given that God had already intervened and shown His power, what do you think Jael's actions reveal about her faith, if anything?

7. Do you think Jael should be commended for her decisiveness, or vilified for what might be construed as betrayal? Explain.

8. A 21st Century woman of purpose will handle adversity quite differently. How do you think Jael's decisiveness translates for today's culture?

Two Hebrew words are translated as "kill" and "murder." One of the words simply describes a killing, without making a moral judgment. This word is used when killing in warfare or judicial execution is involved.

9. What do you think it says about Jael that she was willing to become the warrior, so to speak, at a moment's notice? Do you think this has application today?

Ephesians 6:12 tells us that our battles are not against flesh and blood, but against the rulers, authories, and powers of darkness. Second Corinthians 10:3 reiterates: "For although we are walking in the flesh, we do not wage war in a fleshly way." A faith untamed is required to fight injustice and evil in our world, but 2 Corinthians 10:3-5 makes it clear that we are powerful only through God. In other words, to find the Enemy—the real Villain in the story—requires looking closer; looking beyond "flesh and blood."

Principle for Living

Remember that the results of a faith untamed can have negative repercussions. The actions you take during a crisis will have both short- and long-term consequences. Before you proceed with a decision, make sure your actions align with God's Word. No action contrary to biblical truth is the right choice.

THE FINAL ACT

When Barak arrived in pursuit of Sisera, Jael went out to greet him and said to him, "Come and I will show you the man you are looking for." So he went in with her, and there was Sisera lying dead with a tent peg through his temple!

JUDGES 4:22, HCSB

As Jael wielded her deadly peg and hammer, Barak was in hot pursuit of Sisera. The fact that Jael was quick to share that she killed Israel's greatest foe leaves little doubt of where her personal loyalties lay.

10. Given her husband's neutral political status, why do you think Jael would have taken such a huge risk that could have deeply impacted her marriage?

SINGING A NEW SONG

While Jael's actions may seem alarming to modern readers, it's important to note Deborah's approval of her in this instance. In Judges 5 Deborah poetically praises God for the victory over Sisera's army. She also praises Jael's action:

²⁴*Jael is most blessed of women,*
the wife of Heber the Kenite;
she is most blessed among tent-dwelling women.
²⁵*He asked for water; she gave him milk.*
She brought him curdled milk in a majestic bowl.
²⁶*She reached for a tent peg,*
her right hand, for a workman's mallet.
Then she hammered Sisera —
she crushed his head;
she shattered and pierced his temple.

JUDGES 5:24-26, HCSB

11. The Bible describes Jael as "blessed among tent-dwelling women." Why do you think Scripture holds this opinion of Jael?

Principle for Living

God has equipped you to stand against the Enemy—even in battle. Ask Him daily for discernment, wisdom, and courage. Be vigilant about staying close to Him in the midst of trials.

EMBRACING THE TRUTH

15-20 Minutes

LEADER: *This section focuses on helping group members integrate what they've learned from Jael's story into their own hearts and lives. Invite volunteers to read the Bible passage. Ask women to get into groups of two or three to discuss the following questions.*

1. In what ways, if any, do you think modern Christ followers should strive to be like Jael?

2. Describe a time when you were in a tough spot but waited on God for clear direction. How was your situation helped because you chose to follow God's leading?

3. Describe a time when you took matters into your own hands, didn't wait on God, and people got hurt as a result.

Session Four

4. What do you find most admirable about Jael? Least admirable?

CONNECTING -10-15 *Minutes*

LEADER: Use "Connecting" as a time to deepen the sense of community in your group. The goal is to get to know one another better so that friendships will grow outside this small-group experience.

A prayer partner can be a personal lifeline in tough times. Create two-person prayer teams. Share requests with one another and pray for each other throughout the coming weeks. Keep a journal of prayer requests and answers.

TAKING IT HOME

LEADER: Explain that the "Taking it Home" sections contain introspective questions as well as offering questions to take to God. Encourage each person to set aside quiet time this week so she can make the most of this study and group experience. Be sure to highlight the importance of writing down thoughts, feelings, and key insights that God reveals.

Studying God's truth is not an end in itself. Our goal is always heart and life change. To take the next step of integrating truth into our lives, we need to (1) look honestly into our hearts to understand the true motivations that drive us, and (2) seek God's perspective on our lives. Psalm 51:6 says God "desire[s] truth in the innermost being" (NASB).

A QUESTION TO TAKE TO MY HEART

The following question asks you to look into your heart and focus on your deepest feelings about yourself. Our behaviors are the best indicators of what we really believe deep down. Look deep into the underlying beliefs down in your heart where your truest attitudes and motivations live. Spend some time reflecting, and don't settle for a quick answer.

❧ *What is preventing me from standing against the real enemy—Satan—with the decisiveness of Jael?*

QUESTION TO TAKE TO GOD

When you ask God a question, expect His Spirit to guide your heart to discover His truth. Be careful not to rush or manufacture an answer. Don't write down what you think the "right answer" is. Don't turn the Bible into a spiritual reference book or encyclopedia. Just pose a question to God and wait on Him. Remember, the litmus test for anything we hear from God is alignment with the Bible as our ultimate truth source. Keep a journal of the insights you gain from your time with God.

❧ *Lord, how have you seen me battle the Enemy with the ferocity of Jael?*

SCRIPTURE NOTES

JUDGES 4:11; 15-22

4:11 Heber the Kenite. This Kenite nomad was related to Moses, but he moved his tent in order to sleep with the enemy (v. 17). He likely informed Sisera of Barak's military operations.

4:14 gone before you. Although Deborah herself would not go into battle, the Lord advanced before Barak and his army.

4:18 he went into her tent. As a family friend, Sisera did not consider Jael's warm behavior suspicious.

4:19 gave him a drink. Jael, as was customary in the Middle Eastern rules of hospitality, offered the army captain whatever comforts she could provide.

4:21 hammered the peg into his temple. Used to the customary pitching and tearing down of the tent, Jael skillfully handled her murder weapons. Jael diverted from her husband's allegiance and murdered the captain as Deborah had predicted (v. 9).

4:22 Barak arrived in pursuit of Sisera. The great warrior who was initially reluctant to go to battle came by just in time. To his surprise, he discovered Sisera slain by a woman instead.

JUDGES 5:24-26

5:1-31 Great moments make great songs. Deborah's victory over the Canaanite king is no exception. One of the oldest poems penned in the Bible, the song is full of human emotion. It praises God for his faithfulness. This poem was likely read and sung at a celebration in honor of the victory (Ex. 15:1-18).

SESSION QUOTATIONS

[1]Bible History online. *International Standard Bible Encyclopedia.* Jael. *www.bible-history.com*

A WOMAN
FOR ALL SEASONS

ABIGAIL

Few can read about our next heroine of untamed faith without wondering how a gentle, soft-spoken, beautiful, and intelligent woman could end up married to an awful man like Nabal. Abigail was the wife of Nabal, a man rich by the world's standards but a pauper when it came to character. Chances are she didn't get a vote in this "for worse" pairing. Nabal was a rich rancher, probably much older than Abigail; and it's likely that her father, for reasons we'll never understand, made the miserable match.

Exactly what Abigail had to endure verbally, emotionally, physically, and sexually we shudder to imagine. But even Nabal's dark, suffocating temperament could not extinguish Abigail's determination to live in such a way as to honor God. She walked each day with class and grace, believing even on her darkest days that with God all things are possible. Abigail's story proves that a bad man can't hold a good woman back. The Lord will see her through and will bless her efforts.

BREAKING THE ICE - *15-20 Minutes*

LEADER INSTRUCTIONS FOR THE GROUP EXPERIENCE: This icebreaker is designed to get people talking and keep things moving. Try to keep the tone light-hearted. Don't allow today's session to become a male bashing session. If you have access to one of the following movie titles, you may choose to begin with a clip supporting the "jerk" qualities mentioned:

Many movies revolve around a hateful, vengeful male determined to possess and therefore destroy the life of a sweet, seemingly innocent girl. For instance:

In *Titanic* Cal Hockley (played by Billy Zane) is Rose's egotistical fiancé. His character didn't go down with the ship; but for Rose's sake, you can't help but feel a little disappointed about it.

In *Fried Green Tomatoes* Frank Bennett (played by Nick Searcy) is Ruth's abusive husband. Though she leaves him for her son's safety, he hunts her and threatens revenge.

Hollywood is also fond of playing up the hateful though seemingly pointless ways some selfish and spiteful men interact with other males, too.

In *O Brother, Where Art Thou?* Big Dan Teague (played by John Goodman) is a tree-limb swinging con artist who bullies the movie's main characters.

1. How do you think God feels about bullies?

2. Obviously, bullies are a common theme in our culture. What factors do you think might lead a person to become cruel and mean-spirited?

LEADER: Encourage group members to share a key insight from last session's "Taking it Home." This should only take a couple of minutes, but allow a little more time if it is needed. Affirm those who spent time focusing on their relationship with God this week.

DISCOVERING THE TRUTH

20-25 Minutes

LEADER: In "Discovering the Truth," ask various group members to read the Bible passages aloud. Be sure to leave time for the "Embracing the Truth" and "Connecting" segments that follow this discussion.

SELFISHNESS PERSONIFIED

2A man in Maon had a business in Carmel; he was a very rich man with 3,000 sheep and 1,000 goats and was shearing his sheep in Carmel. 3The man's name was Nabal, and his wife's name, Abigail. The woman was intelligent and beautiful, but the man, a Calebite, was harsh and evil in his dealings.

1 SAMUEL 25:2-3, HCSB

As far as we can tell, Nabal didn't possess a single redeeming quality. He was greedy, mean, selfish, and apparently liked to pick fights. Undoubtedly he treated his wife as a possession and slave.

LEADER: Discuss as many discovery questions as time permits. Encourage participation by inviting different individuals to respond. Differing perspectives will enrich your discussions. It will help to highlight in advance the questions you don't want to miss. Be familiar with the "Scripture Notes" at the end of this session.

1. Consider what daily life must have been like for Abigail. How do you think she coped with her unpleasant husband?

2. Do you think a woman in Abigail's position would have sought a divorce? Why or why not?

Session Five

In 1 Samuel 24–25:1, David has been through emotional turmoil. He has been chased around by King Saul and his men, who are convinced David is plotting to kill Saul. When David has his chance to do away with his kingly superior, he balks and comes face-to-face with the king. David explains that although his men desired that he kill the king, he would not take out God's anointed. In verse 1 of chapter 25, we discover that the prophet Samuel had died. Samuel was not only a mentor to David, but also the man who anointed him king. David's experiences in Nabal's territory are immediately after Samuel's funeral. Certainly after this tumultuous time, David was hoping to avoid adversity and find someone more accommodating.

⁴While David was in the wilderness, he heard that Nabal was shearing sheep, ⁵so David sent 10 young men instructing them, "Go up to Carmel, and when you come to Nabal, greet him in my name. ⁶Then say this: 'Long life to you, and peace to you, to your family, and to all that is yours. ⁷I hear that you are shearing. When your shepherds were with us, we did not harass them, and nothing of theirs was missing the whole time they were in Carmel. ⁸Ask your young men, and they will tell you. So let my young men find favor with you, for we have come on a feast day. Please give whatever you can afford to your servants and to your son David.'"

⁹David's young men went and said all these things to Nabal on David's behalf, and they waited.

1 SAMUEL 25:4-9, HCSB

When David and his band of brothers had set up camp near Nabal's ranch, marauders kept clear of the rancher's livestock. As a direct result of their presence, Nabal prospered. It was a custom of the day to offer hospitality to such guardians as an expression of grace and gratitude. Nabal, however, snubbed custom. Perhaps he felt that if David and his men wanted food, they should pay for it just like everyone else.

¹⁰Nabal asked them, "Who is David? Who is Jesse's son? Many slaves these days are running away from their masters. ¹¹Am I supposed to take my bread, my water, and my meat that I butchered for my shearers and give them to men who are from I don't know where?"

1 SAMUEL 25:10-11, HCSB

Nabal may have been rich, but he certainly lacked in the common sense department. With his arrogant words and selfish behavior, he gravely insulted the region's most revered warrior—a man who took out a giant with a rock and slingshot.

Session Five

12David's men retraced their steps. When they returned to him, they reported all these words. 13He said to his men, "All of you, put on your swords!" So David and all his men put on their swords. About 400 men followed David while 200 stayed with the supplies.

1 SAMUEL 25:12-13, HCSB

3. How do you think Nabal became so disagreeable? What circumstances do you think made him so sick at heart?

Principle for Living
God calls us to treat others as we would like to be treated. If someone makes a reasonable request of your help, offer it with a willing heart.

WISDOM DIFFUSES THE FOOL'S DAMAGE

The servants who heard Nabal tell David's men to take a hike probably backed slowly out of the vicinity and then ran to pack their bags. It was time to get out of town! Nabal had just insulted the Giant Killer, and they weren't waiting around for the rocks to start flying.

One smart young man, however, ran straight to Abigail, who was probably busily preparing food for the celebration feast. As the sweat poured off his brow, he didn't mince words:

14"Look, David sent messengers from the wilderness to greet our master, but he yelled at them. 15The men treated us well. When we were in the field, we weren't harassed and nothing of ours was missing the whole time we were living among them. 16They were a wall around us, both day and night, the entire time we were herding the sheep. 17Now consider carefully what you must do, because there is certain to be trouble for our master and his entire family. He is such a worthless fool nobody can talk to him!"

1 SAMUEL 25:14B-17, HCSB

The servant's breathless report was probably nothing new to Abigail. Most likely it was a familiar place for her. She kept her cool and shifted into peacekeeping mode.

18Abigail hurried, taking 200 loaves of bread, two skins of wine, five butchered sheep, a bushel of roasted grain, 100 clusters of raisins, and 200 cakes of pressed figs, and loaded them on donkeys. 19Then she said to her male servants, "Go ahead of me. I will be right behind you." But she did not tell her husband Nabal.

1 SAMUEL 25:18-19, HCSB

4. What does this passage tell you about Abigail's self-control? Her ability to make decisions under pressure?

5. How do you think Abigail's reaction represents a faith untamed? In what ways do you think this solution is admirable?

A WAY WITH WORDS

Abigail must have had someone in her life who taught her that words well spoken are like gold. Maybe a female mentor, an older woman of untamed faith, showed Abigail how to influence others with patience, a loving touch, and words aptly delivered. Perhaps she simply learned the tactics through repeated run-ins with Nabal's mean spirit and selfish pride. Regardless of its source, Abigail had an undeniable ability to negotiate peace. Her words would enable David to retain his self-respect and the respect of his men as she appealed to his political goals and moral commitments.

20As [Abigail] rode the donkey down a mountain pass hidden from view, she saw David and his men coming toward her and met them. 21David had just said, "I guarded everything that belonged to this man in the wilderness for nothing. He was not missing anything, yet he paid me back evil for good. 22May God punish me, and even more if I let any of his men survive until morning."

23When Abigail saw David, she quickly got off the donkey and fell with her face to the ground in front of David. 24She fell at his feet and said, "The guilt is mine, my lord, but please let your servant speak to you directly. Listen to the words of your servant. 25My lord should pay no attention to this worthless man Nabal, for he lives up to his name: His name is Nabal, and stupidity is all he knows. I, your servant, didn't see my lord's young men whom you sent. 26Now my lord, as surely as the LORD lives and as you yourself live, it is the LORD who kept you from participating in bloodshed and avenging yourself by your own hand. May your enemies and those who want trouble for my lord be like Nabal. 27Accept this gift your servant has brought to my lord, and let it be given to the young men who follow my lord. 28Please forgive your servant's offense, for the LORD is certain to make a lasting dynasty for my lord because he fights the LORDs battles. Throughout your life, may evil not be found in you.

29"When someone pursues you and attempts to take your life, my lord's life will be tucked safely in the place where the LORD your God protects the living. However, He will fling away your enemies' lives like stones from a sling. 30When the LORD does for my lord all the good He promised and appoints you ruler over Israel, 31there will not be remorse or a troubled conscience for my lord because of needless bloodshed or my lord's revenge. And when the LORD does good things for my lord, may you remember me your servant."

1 SAMUEL 25:20-31, HCSB

By siding with David and physically meeting his original request for food, Abigail demonstrated savvy peacekeeping skills. Scan First Samuel 25:23-31 above for specific things Abigail said or did that helped to salvage David's pride and earn his respect. *Underline them.*

THANK GOD FOR SMART WOMEN

Surely Abigail's God-given physical beauty caught David's attention when he was on the warpath, but it was her intelligence and tone that turned his hand from the intended bloodshed that would have dishonored him and angered God.

³²Then David said to Abigail, "Praise to the LORD God of Israel, who sent you to meet me today! ³³Blessed is your discernment, and blessed are you. Today you kept me from participating in bloodshed and avenging myself by my own hand. ³⁴Otherwise, as surely as the LORD God of Israel lives, who prevented me from harming you, if you had not come quickly to meet me, Nabal wouldn't have had any men left by morning light." ³⁵Then David accepted what she had brought him and said, "Go home in peace. See, I have heard what you said and have granted your request."

1 SAMUEL 25:32-35, HCSB

6. How do you think Abigail's actions honored both David and Nabal while at the same time allowing her to maintain self-respect?

Session Five

Principle for Living
When we've offended someone, we are wise to quickly seek their forgiveness and make amends.

THE BEAST GOES BELLY UP

When Abigail turned her donkey toward home, her peacekeeping plan was only half complete. Even though Nabal wasn't worthy of honor, Abigail submitted to his authority as her husband. She chose to tell Nabal what she had done, but she was careful to time her words.

7. In what ways do you think Abigail has honored Nabal in this confrontation with David?

In his book, *What Paul Really Said About Women*, John Temple Bistrow translates the biblical expectation of a spouse as the voluntary act of allegiance and support while also responding to the needs of the other.[1]

8. What elements do you think might be missing from the expectations given in Bistrow's book?

9. While hardly romantic or inspiring, Bistrow's expectations probably represent the conclusions of many. Do you think Nabal meets these minimum requirements? Abigail?

10. If the marriage relationship is in any way similar to our relationship with God, how do you think these expectations apply to your divine relationship with God?

Session Five

Unfortunately for Nabal, Abigail's quick thinking only delayed Nabal's ultimate fate.

36Then Abigail went to Nabal, and there he was in his house, feasting like a king. Nabal was in a good mood and very drunk, so she didn't say anything to him until morning light.

37In the morning when Nabal sobered up, his wife told him about these events. Then he had a seizure and became paralyzed. 38About 10 days later, the LORD struck Nabal dead.

1 SAMUEL 25:36-38, HCSB

11. What do you think Nabal's illness and death reveal about the consequences of a life of bitterness, hardness, and bullying?

Principle for Living

*Abigail took action to preserve the life of her husband and the
lives of the other members of her household. Sometimes our love
for family is best demonstrated through selflessness.*

CONFIDENT MEN LOVE STRONG WOMEN

Abigail's story does not conclude with her becoming a widow. On the
contrary, she is quickly claimed by another. The moment he learned of
Nabal's death, David sent messengers requesting Abigail's hand in marriage.

*³⁹When David heard that Nabal was dead, he said, "Praise the LORD who championed
my cause against Nabal's insults and restrained His servant from doing evil. The LORD
brought Nabal's evil deeds back on his own head."*

*Then David sent messengers to speak to Abigail about marrying him. ⁴⁰When David's
servants came to Abigail at Carmel, they said to her, "David sent us to bring you to him
as a wife."*

*⁴¹She bowed her face to the ground and said, "Here I am, your servant, to wash the feet of
my lord's servants."*

1 SAMUEL 25:39-41, HCSB

Likely David viewed Abigail as a woman who could complement
his own strengths and help to balance his weaknesses.

12. Although it's unlikely Abigail had any choice in the selection of her first
marriage partner, she did have the option to refuse David's offer. Why
do you think she said yes so quickly? Before you respond, consider
that Nabal had left her quite wealthy with a household of servants
at her disposal.

Principle for Living

*God sees our hearts as we make decisions that honor
Him. He will provide for our futures.*

Session Five

EMBRACING THE TRUTH
15-20 Minutes

LEADER: *This section focuses on helping group members integrate what they've learned from the Bible into their own hearts and lives. Invite volunteers to read the Bible passages.*

Abigail's story opens a vital window to understanding how Christ-followers should respond to persecution—particularly from unbelieving spouses. Christian counselors Tim Jackson and Jeff Olson offer this vital and potentially life-saving principle for living:

> *In the case of abuse ... a loving and submissive wife is called to be engaged in doing what she can to 'save' and preserve the life of her spouse. This is submitting to (aligning herself under) God's good purposes for him as a man and fulfilling God's design for her as a woman.*
>
> *What does it look like to "do what is right"? Rather than tolerating abuse, a biblically submissive and loving wife will creatively learn to be as shrewd as a snake and as innocent as a dove in exposing him and letting others know about the destructiveness of his abuse, and to invite him to know the goodness of God's mercy. ... She will be motivated by her loving respect for him because she believes in his potential of becoming the kind of loving man he could be if he submitted to Christ's leadership in his life.[2]*

1. How do you think a woman's strength can be best utilized in a relationship like Abigail had with Nabal?

2. Isaiah 41:10 says, *"Do not fear, for I am with you; do not be afraid, for I am your God. I will strengthen you; I will help you; I will hold on to you with My righteous right hand"* (HCSB). In what ways do you think an untamed faith like Abigail's can be wise counsel in an abusive situation?

Session Five

Understand that the Bible is very much against abuse of any sort. If you are in an abusive relationship, please visit *www.abigail-ministries.org*, a support group for women with abusive partners.

Principle for Living
God doesn't promise to always deliver us from every difficulty, but He does promise to redeem and remain with us through adversity.

CONNECTING *-10-15 Minutes*

LEADER: Use "Connecting" as a time to begin to bond with, encourage, and support one another. Physical, emotional, and verbal abuse is not uncommon in Christian marriage but is often kept secret due to feeling fear and shame. Ask women to join hands. Lead the group in prayer, asking God to give anyone in an abusive relationship the courage to wisely and safely ask for help. Also ask God to help the women in this small group recognize the symptoms of abuse and to have the courage to wisely and safely reach out to help.

Share and record group prayer requests that you will regularly pray over between now and the next session.

PRAYER REQUESTS:

TAKING IT HOME

LEADER: For this week's "Taking it Home" activity, invite each person in your group to identify a location that's special to her. Perhaps there's a special room, stream, garden, or lake. For some, a bubble bath or sun room will do the trick. Encourage ladies to meet with God in that special place to discuss their questions for their hearts and for God.

QUESTIONS TO TAKE TO MY HEART

This is introspection time—time to grapple with what drives your thinking and behavior, to understand what you really believe in your innermost being about God, yourself, and the world in which you live. Your behavior—not your intellectual stance—is the best indicator of your true beliefs.

❧ *How do I often respond when others treat me poorly? What peace-keeping traits can I begin to model this week?*

Session Five

Question to Take to God

When you ask God a question, expect His Spirit to guide your heart to discover His truth. Be careful not to rush or manufacture an answer. Don't write down what you think the "right answer" is. Don't turn the Bible into a spiritual reference book or encyclopedia. Just pose a question to God and wait on Him. Remember, the litmus test for anything we hear from God is alignment with the Bible as our ultimate truth source. Keep a journal of the insights you gain from your time with God.

    ❧ *Lord, are there areas of my relationships in which I fail to honor You?*

Scripture Notes

1 SAMUEL 25:2-41

25:2-44 Nabal. His name meant "fool." He certainly dealt with David foolishly. This passage describes a husband who was as foolish as his wife was wise. Abigail saved the situation, but Nabal didn't survive it.

25:8 Please give. Nabal insulted David by refusing his request. David's men could have plundered Nabal's flocks easily. Nabal's smarter choice would have been to help the renegade leader.

25:22 punish me, and even more. This is a severe Hebrew curse. David's oath of revenge reveals the other side of his leadership: quick, sure, confident, and violent.

25:25 His name is Nabal. The name "Nabal" meant "fool." Names often reflect the character of a person, especially during this era. That's why God often changed a person's name after he or she passed a pivotal point. Even in the New Testament, names are significant. In the book of Philemon, Paul makes a request based on the meaning of a name. He asks that Onesimus (whose name means "useful" or "profitable") be made useful again (Philem. 1:10-11).

25:28 may evil not be found in you. Abigail was a clever diplomat. She appealed to David's legacy, integrity, and reputation. David's passion was not indifferent to all this cleverness, and eventually Abigail became his wife (v. 42).

25:29 in the place where the LORD your God protects the living. In other words, God will keep you safe and alive. *like stones from a sling.* An apt image given David's victory over Goliath.

25:32 Praise to the LORD. David could see with spiritual eyes. Abigail had provided supplies for his men and kept him from an error in judgment and needless bloodshed.

25:36 in a good mood and very drunk. Nabal (fool) was all that his name implied. Even while his wife was saving the farm, he was partying.

25:37 became paralyzed. Perhaps a heart attack or stroke.

ISAIAH 41:10

41:10 Do not fear ... do not be afraid. God will be with Abraham's descendants (Deut. 31:6), bringing them back from the exile. He punished Israel, but He did not cast her away.

SESSION QUOTATIONS

[1] John Temple Bristow, *What Paul Really Said About Women*, (San Francisco: Harper Collins, San Francisco, 1991).

[2] Tim Jackson and Jeff Olson, *When Violence Comes Home: Help for Victims of Spouse Abuse* (Grand Rapids, MI: Radio Bible Class).

IN THE COMPANY OF WOMEN

WHEN GODLY WOMEN GET TOGETHER GOOD THINGS HAPPEN

For the past five weeks you've been in the company of four biblical heroines. You have spent time with Rahab, Deborah, Jael, and Abigail by heart — what makes them tick and what ticks them off. You are familiar with their strengths and weaknesses, their triumphs and tragedies, their loves and losses. These four ladies persevered through the most difficult of circumstances. Even though they lived thousands of years ago, their faith legacy lives on.

Every woman who follows Christ has the potential to do great things for Him. Christ wants to shine His love through us. That means that you too can be a warrior for His cause — perhaps not on the battlefield, but definitely through your interactions with others. When women who love the Lord get together, good things happen. Burdens are shared. Hope grows. Faith is encouraged. Learn to use your time with other believers to grow in your appreciation of Christ, and don't be afraid to let His love shine through you!

BREAKING THE ICE - *20 Minutes*

LEADER INSTRUCTIONS FOR THE GROUP EXPERIENCE:
This icebreaker should be fun. To prepare for this session, bring tear sheets and markers and purchase or borrow Liz Curtis Higgs' book, **Bad Girls of the Bible.** *Scan the content to learn the personality traits of four bad but powerful women. Select one to be a political candidate and three others as her campaign team. Create a quick-read summary for each of the women on the "Bad Girls" political team. Explain that these "Bad Girls" will be running against God's choice for Governor of the great state of Shenanigans.*

As a group, choose a political candidate from one of the four women studied in *Faith Untamed*. She will run against a "Bad Girl of the Bible" to win the office of Governor of fictitious state of Shenanigans. List on a tear sheet her qualifications based on the things you've learned about her temperament, talents, and skills.

Place the remaining women from *Faith Untamed* into the following key roles on the candidate's campaign team.

Candidate for Governor of Shenanigans:

Campaign Manager:

Security Chief:

Press Secretary:

1. Create a campaign platform for your candidate that explains how this choice will best serve the state of Shenanigans.

2. Compare and contrast the two political teams before declaring a winner.

LEADER: Encourage participants to share a key insight from last week's "Taking it Home" questions.

DISCOVERING THE TRUTH
15-20 Minutes

LEADER: For "Discovering the Truth," ask for volunteers to read the roles of Rahab, Deborah, Jael, and Abigail. Be sure to leave time for the "Embracing the Truth" and "Connecting" segments that follow this discussion.

What if Rahab, Deborah, Jael, and Abigail could spend time together? How do you think it would go? Read along and answer the following questions.

Deborah: Jael, thanks so much for being our hostess. Love this rug by the way! It's the *replacement rug* isn't it?

Jael: Yes, I couldn't look at that stained carpet a moment longer. Too many memories. A trader came by the tent but the price tag just about blew my sandals off. I finally managed a deal without having to give up everything we've worked so hard for.

Goat's milk anyone?

Deborah, Rahab, and Abigail trade glances and then burst out laughing.

Rahab: You always get the deals! By the way, do you ever regret taking things into your own hands that day?

Jael: Yes and no. Sisera was a bad man. The stories of how he tortured, raped, and murdered people still send chills down my spine. And I was raised to be tough. I was taught at early age to take action.

Rahab: But...

Jael: Should I have waited and let Barak handle the situation? I ask myself that question a lot. In fact it haunts me. Sometimes there just aren't easy answers.

Rahab: And sometimes there's more time to make a decision than other times. I just knew that I wanted more and God was the only way for me.

Jael: (Pauses for a moment) Yes. To be honest, here's where I am. I try each day to rely more on God and less on me. Although I'm not ashamed of what I did—which doesn't make it any easier—I can say that I've learned a lot about who I am through these times. God has also used the experience to reveal Himself.

Deborah: We've all grown wiser because of tough times. (She rises and wraps her arms around Jael.) You'll always be a hero to me, Jael. Know that.

Rahab: People do tag us for the past, don't they? I've been married to Salmon for 20 years, but some women still sneer behind my back because of my former occupation. I'm so thankful God doesn't dig up bones the way people do.

Deborah: Speaking of old bones, Abigail, was life with Nabal simply horrible?

Abigail: Nabal was a brutal man. Trust me, there were moments I wanted to kill him; but I think God protected my heart, and to be honest, I was just too stubborn to let Nabal steal my joy. Then along came David, so the opposite of Nabal. Not perfect, but the right man for me. David loves me; he adores my mind, celebrates my intelligence, and values my opinion.

Rahab: I'm still amazed that Salmon saw me for the woman I could be—not just the woman I was. He gave our son Boaz that same eye for true beauty. Who would have ever thought I would be surrounded by so much true and tender love? God is so good.

Abigail: Deborah, will you please answer a question I think we've all asked ourselves at one time or another? Do you ever get tired of being a warrior for the Lord and just want to go back to life as usual?

Deborah: (Throws back her head and laughs.) More often than you can even imagine! Then I look at my daughter and know that as one of God's strong girls, I've got to press on. I have the obligation to help my daughter become the woman God wants her be, to teach her through my strengths and my weaknesses. To lead by example so that she will never underestimate what God can do and will do through her if her heart remains willing.

Living a life of untamed faith is my legacy to her. It hasn't been easy, but it has been worth the struggle. My prayer is that my daughter will always remember me as a woman who loved God completely, a woman who didn't cower but lived her faith out loud—untamed, unashamed, undaunted. And you know something, girls? I've got a feeling that God will use all of us to tell His story of untamed faith. The story of how He chooses the least likely people to do the most amazing things.

LEADER: Discuss as many "Discovery Questions" as time permits. It will help to highlight in advance the questions you don't want to miss. Be familiar with the "Scripture Notes" at the end of this session.

1. Jael and Deborah were contemporaries, but Abigail and Rahab lived in different eras. Do you believe, had they been given the chance to chat, that they would've had fellowship as is described in the dramatic sketch? Why or why not?

2. What commonalities do our four women of *Faith Untamed* share?

3. What is the value of godly women hanging out together? Is such fellowship important? Explain.

God doesn't make mistakes, nor does He allow DNA to weave its own way by chance. He creates each woman with unique personality traits, special skills, and individual quirks for reasons all His own. Just as He created Rahab, Deborah, Jael, and Abigail to accomplish things for His glory, He created you for a unique purpose. He can use you to tell others about Him and to encourage others in Him.

Becoming a woman of untamed faith begins in understanding how and why God created us. Consider your unique design as you listen to the words of Psalm 139.

¹Lord, You have searched me and known me.
²You know when I sit down and when I stand up;
You understand my thoughts from far away.
³You observe my travels and my rest;
You are aware of all my ways.
⁴Before a word is on my tongue,
You know all about it, Lord.
⁵You have encircled me;
You have placed Your hand on me.
¹³For it was You who created my inward parts;
You knit me together in my mother's womb.
¹⁴I will praise You,
because I have been remarkably and wonderfully made.
Your works are wonderful,
and I know this very well.
¹⁵My bones were not hidden from You
when I was made in secret,
when I was formed in the depths of the earth.
¹⁶Your eyes saw me when I was formless;
all my days were written in Your book and planned
before a single one of them began.

PSALM 139:1-5,13-16, HCSB

Jeremiah 29:11 states, " *'For I know the plans I have for you,' declares the Lord,*
'plans … to give you hope and a future' " (NIV). Every follower of Christ has
purpose. A large part of that purpose is to tell others about Him, both
through active evangelism and through letting our lives shine as a light.

4. How might the knowledge that God knew you before you were born and
that He plans to give you a future help you live a faith untamed?

5. Why is it important that we know what the Bible has to say about our
purpose as God's children?

> ### *Principle for Living*
> *A faith untamed puts aside the fear that paralyzes a woman of purpose. A faith untamed is not subject to the status quo, only the direction and leading of God.*

EMBRACING THE TRUTH
15-20 Minutes

LEADER: *This section focuses on helping group members integrate what they've learned from the Bible into their own hearts and lives. Prior to the meeting, ask group members to flip through magazines and find pictures of women that match their mental images of Rahab, Deborah, Jael, and Abigail. Ask them to bring the pictures to the group meeting. Compare the different perceptions each woman has of Rahab, Deborah, Jael, and Abigail. On tear sheets, list the personality traits of each of these women. Glue the magazines photos to the appropriate tear sheets. Then discuss the following questions.*

Consider the women you've met in *Faith Untamed*.
Recall the personality traits of each as you answer the following:

The woman I most relate to is _____ because …

The woman I most admire is _____ because …

If I could spend the day with one of these women, I would love to get to know _____ better because …

I think _____ and _____ would have been best friends if they had lived at the same time because …

If I ran around with _____ we could get into a lot of trouble but we would have a lot of laughs.

I think the thing that God most liked about

Rahab was her _____;

Deborah was her _____;

Jael was her _____;

Abigail was her _____.

I think what God most likes about me is _____.

Of the women we've studied, I am most like _____ and least like _____.

What I like most about Rahab is _____.

What I like most about Deborah is _____.

What I like most about Jael is _____.

What I like most about Abigail is _____.

What I like most about myself is _____.

The question I think these women would ask me, as a modern follower of God, is _____.

The company of other women often unveils truths about us. Learning how other women navigate tough times can often inspire us to have the faith and courage to take risks we otherwise would not take.

Through studying the untamed faith of Rahab, Deborah, Jael, and Abigail, I have learned that I _____.

CONNECTING - *10 Minutes*

LEADER: Read aloud the following to the group: "We women are a wonderful creation of God. He loves the way we look, think, talk, smell, laugh, love, and multi-task our way through life. He wants to encourage us in our walk with Him. Often He'll do that through the words of others." Distribute a set of colored cards to each person. The name of each woman in your group should be written on a separate card within the set so that every woman has a full collection of names, excluding her own.

Write a note of encouragement to each woman in the group, noting her God-given strengths. When you are finished, hand the cards to their owners.

LEADER: Before you close, ask the women to join stand shoulder-to-shoulder with their arms around each other. Explain that sometimes we hear God's "Atta Girls" and other times we don't, but He always hears our prayers. Read aloud the following passages of Scripture as edited and compiled by author, Beth Moore.

> *Oh, the depths of the riches, both of Your wisdom, Lord, and Your knowledge. How unsearchable are Your judgments and untraceable Your ways (Romans 11:33). It is by Your grace and Your grace alone that I am what I am (1 Corinthians 15:10), for from You, and through you, and to You are all things. To You be the glory forever, precious Lord (Romans 11:36).*

TAKING IT HOME

LEADER: "Taking it Home" this week focuses on your legacy as a Christ-follower. Encourage each person to set aside quiet time this week so she can make the most of this study and group experience. Be sure to highlight the importance of journaling.

This is introspection time—time to grapple with what drives your thinking and behavior, to understand what you really believe in your innermost being about God, yourself, and the world in which you live. Your behavior—not your intellectual stance—is the best indicator of your true beliefs.

QUESTION TO TAKE TO MY HEART

The following question asks you to look into your heart and focus on your deepest feelings about yourself. Our behaviors are the best indicators of what we really believe deep down. Look deep into the underlying beliefs down in your heart where your truest attitudes and motivations live. Spend some time reflecting, and don't settle for a quick answer.

❧ *What are the lies that keep my strength stowed neatly away and out of the fight against the real Enemy?*

QUESTION TO TAKE TO GOD

When you ask God a question, expect His Spirit to guide your heart to discover His truth. Be careful not to rush or manufacture an answer. Don't write down what you think the "right answer" is. Don't turn the Bible into a spiritual reference book or encyclopedia. Just pose a question to God and wait on Him. Remember, the litmus test for anything we hear from God is alignment with the Bible as our ultimate truth source. Keep a journal of the insights you gain from your time with God.

❧ *God, in what areas of my life can I live with a greater sense of power in You?*

SCRIPTURE NOTES

PSALM 139:1-5,13-16

Psalm 139 All Knowing, Ever Present.
God is not being presented as merely
the all-knowing, all-seeing God that
intimidates by His knowledge. Rather,
God is presented as deeply personal
and deeply caring of the birth and life
of each individual.

139:13 You who created. God is the One
who creates the unique mental and
physical attributes of each individual.
This implies loving care for each detail
of our own complexity.

139:16 Your eyes saw. God sees absolutely
everything. He even sees every human
being as he or she is being formed
in the womb. God has determined
the length of each person's life. The
blueprint for everything is in the mind
of God.

Notes

Notes

LEADER'S GUIDE

Leader Guide

DISCOVER PURPOSE THROUGH THE JOURNEY
WITH OTHER COMPELLING STUDIES IN THE
WOMEN OF PURPOSE SERIES!

REQUIRED SUPPLIES AND PREPARATION FOR EACH SESSION

*We do not approve of every word, action, or scene in the movies we have chosen to be a part of this Women of Purpose experience. Please review each clip for suitability in your specific situation.

SESSION 1:

Supplies: - DVD of *The Sandlot** (1993, 2003 on DVD)

     - TV/DVD player

     - Toilet paper and felt-tip pens

     - Colorful 4x6 index cards

Procedure:
Show chapter 13, "A Challenge" (44:00 to 46:45 on the DVD timer), of *The Sandlot* after question 1 of "Breaking the Ice." Then discuss questions. Warn the group of some language that might be considered crass.

Before "Discovering the Truth," show chapter 22, "Benny's Dream (1:14:17 to 1:17:39 on the DVD timer), of *The Sandlot*.

In "Connecting," you will have the women write down negative thoughts they have about themselves on the paper and then ceremonially dispose them. After that activity and reading the paragraph that follows, lead the participants in writing the listed Bible verses on your index cards, placing their own names where there
is a blank.

SESSION 2:

Supplies: - Two red cords or ribbons for each woman

Procedure:
During "Connecting," give each woman two red cords or lengths of ribbon. Instruct them to use one as a bookmark in her Bible to remember the vital importance of living by faith each day. Ask them to hold onto the other one during the prayer in honor of a family member who does not know Christ.

Preparation

SESSION 3:

Supplies: - DVD of *Stars Wars Episode IV: A New Hope** (1977, starring Carrie Fisher, Harrison Ford, Mark Hamill)

- TV/DVD player

Procedure:
Before beginning "Breaking the Ice," show chapter 26, "Alderaan's Fate," (57:00 to 59:10 on the DVD timer) of *Star Wars*. You may also show a clip from chapter 32, "Rescuing the Princess," for additional illustration: 1:14:11 to 1:19:04. Then discuss the three questions in "Breaking the Ice."

SESSION 4:

Supplies: - CD or other recording of The Carpenters' song "Rainy Days and Mondays" (from the album *The Carpenters*, 1971)

- CD/tape/MP3 player

Procedure:
Before "Breaking the Ice," play "Rainy Days and Mondays" for your group, and then discuss the questions.

SESSION 5:

Supplies: - If desired, DVD of *Titanic*, *Fried Green Tomatoes*, or *O Brother, Where Art Thou?** and DVD player

Procedure:
If you have easy access to one of the movies listed above, prepare to show a clip of the "bad boy" the author talks about in "Breaking the Ice." Show the clip either before "Breaking the Ice" or after you talk about that particular bad boy.

Ask women to bring pictures from magazines that fit their images of Rahab, Deborah, Jael, and Abigal for session 6.

Possible clip from *Titanic*, *Fried Green Tomatoes*, or *O Brother, Where Art Thou?*

Preparation

SESSION 6:

Supplies: - tear sheets and markers

         - colored 4x6 index cards

         - pictures from magazines that fit womens' images of Rahab, Deborah, Jael, and Abigal

         - glue or glue sticks

Procedure:

Before the session, scan Liz Curtis Higgs' book *Bad Girls of the Bible*. On a tear sheet, write out the personality traits and names of four of the "bad girls." Before "Breaking the Ice," explain to your group that these Bad Girls will be running against God's choice for Governor of the State of Shenanigans. Then follow the instructions in questions 1–4.

During "Embracing the Truth," have women get out their magazine cut-outs. As a group, list personality traits of each woman you've studied on a separate tear sheet. Then have women glue their pictures to the bottom of the tear sheets. Continue answering the "Embracing the Truth" questions.

Before the session, you will need to make a set of note cards for each woman in your study. Each note card should have one participant's name on it. Make a complete set for each woman—everyone should have everyone else's name except her own. Distribute these for the "Connecting" segment. Invite participants to write a note of encouragement to the other women in the study on the note cards, and then give the cards to their owners.

Preparation

Leading a Small Group

You will find a great deal of helpful information in this section that will be crucial for success as you lead your group.

Reading through this and utilizing the suggested principles and practices will greatly enhance the group experience. You need to accept the limitations of leadership. You cannot transform a life. You must lead your group to the Bible, the Holy Spirit, and the power of Christian community. By doing so your group will have all the tools necessary to draw closer to God and each other and to experiencing heart transformation.

Make the following things available at each session:
- *Faith Untamed* book for each attendee
- Bible for each attendee
- Snacks and refreshments
- Pens or pencils for each attendee

THE SETTING AND GENERAL TIPS:

1. Prepare for each meeting by reviewing the material, praying for each group member, asking the Holy Spirit to join you, and making Jesus the centerpiece of every experience.

2. Create the right environment by making sure chairs are arranged so each person can see the eyes of every other attendee. Set the room temperature at 69 degrees. If meeting in a home, make sure pets are in a location where they cannot interrupt the meeting. Request that cell phones are turned off unless someone is expecting an emergency call. Have music playing as people arrive (volume low enough for people to converse) and, if possible, burn a sweet-smelling candle.

3. Try to have soft drinks and coffee available for early arrivals.

4. Have someone with the spiritual gift of hospitality ready to make any new attendees feel welcome.

5. Be sure there is adequate lighting so that everyone can read without straining.

6. Connect with group members away from group time. The amount of participation you have during your group meetings is directly related to the amount of time you connect with your group members away from the meeting time.

7. There are four types of questions used in each session: Observation (What is the passage telling us?), Interpretation (What does the passage mean?), Self-revelation (How am I doing in light of the truth unveiled?), and Application (Now that I know what I know, what will I do to integrate this truth into my life?). You won't be able to use all the questions in each study, but be sure to use some from each.

8. Don't get impatient about the depth of relationship group members are experiencing. Building real Christian Community takes time.

9. Be sure pens and/or pencils are available for attendees at each meeting.

10. Never ask someone to pray aloud without first getting her permission.

LEADING MEETINGS:

1. Before the icebreakers, do not say, "Now we're going to do an icebreaker." The meeting should feel like a conversation from beginning to end, not a classroom experience.

2. Be certain every member responds to the icebreaker questions. The goal is for every person to hear her own voice early in the meeting. People will then feel comfortable to converse later on. If members can't think of a response, let them know you'll come back to them after the others have spoken.

3. Remember, a great group leader talks less than 10% of the time. If you ask a question and no one answers, just wait. If you create an environment where you fill the gaps of silence, the group will quickly learn they needn't join you in the conversation.

4. Don't be hesitant to call people by name as you ask them to respond to questions or to give their opinions. Be sensitive, but engage everyone in the conversation.

5. Don't ask people to read aloud unless you have gotten their permission prior to the meeting. Feel free to ask for volunteers to read.

6. Watch your time. If discussion time is extending past the time limits suggested, offer the option of pressing on into other discussions or continuing the current session into your next meeting. REMEMBER: People and their needs are always more important than completing all the questions.

THE GROUP:

Each small group has its own persona. Every group is made up of a unique set of personalities, backgrounds, and life experiences. This diversity creates a dynamic distinctive to that specific group of people. Embracing the unique character of your group and the individuals in that group is vital to group members experiencing all you're hoping for.

Treat each person as a special, responsible, and valuable member of this Christian community. By doing so you'll bring out the best in each of them, thus creating a living, breathing, life-changing group dynamic.

YOU CAN HELP GROUP MEMBERS THROUGH ...

Support – Provide plenty of time for support among the group members. Encourage members to connect with each other between meetings when necessary.

Shared Feelings – Reassure the members that their feelings are very normal in a situation such as they are in. Encourage the members to share their feelings with one another.

Advice Giving – Avoid giving advice. Encourage cross-talk (members talking to each other), but limit advice giving. "Should" and "ought to" statements tend to increase the guilt the loss has already created.

Silence – Silence is not a problem. Even though it may seem awkward, silence is just a sign that people are not ready to talk. It DOES NOT mean they aren't thinking or feeling. If the silence needs to be broken, be sure you break it with the desire to move forward.

Prayer – Prayer is vital to personal and community growth. Starting and ending with prayer is important. However, people may need prayer in the middle of the session. Here's a way to know when the time is right to pray. If a member is sharing and you sense a need to pray, then begin to look for a place to add it.

Welcome to Community!

Meeting together with a group of people to study God's Word and experience life together is an exciting adventure. A small group is ... *a group of people unwilling to settle for anything less than redemptive community.*

Core Values

Community: God is relational, so He created us to live in relationship with Him and each other. Authentic community involves *sharing life together* and *connecting* on many levels with the people in our group.

Group Process: Developing authentic community requires a step-by-step process. It's a journey of sharing our stories with each other and learning together.

Stages of Development: Every healthy group goes through *various* stages as it matures over a period of months or years. We begin with the *birth* of a new group, deepen our relationships in the *growth* and *development* stages, and ultimately *multiply* to form other new groups.

Interactive Bible Study: God provided the Bible as an instruction manual of life. We need to deepen our understanding of God's Word. People learn and remember more as they wrestle with truth and learn from others. The process of Bible discovery and group interaction will enhance our growth.

Experiential Growth: The goal of studying the Bible together is not merely a quest for knowledge; this should result in real life change. Beyond solely reading, studying, and dissecting the Bible, being a disciple of Christ involves reunifying knowledge with experience. We do this by bringing our questions to God, opening a dialogue with our hearts (instead of killing our desires), and utilizing other ways to listen to God speak to us (group interaction, nature, art, movies, circumstances, etc.). Experiential growth is always grounded in the Bible as God's primary means of revelation and our ultimate truth-source.

Power of God: Our processes and strategies will be ineffective unless we invite and embrace the presence and power of God. In order to experience community and growth, Jesus needs to be the centerpiece of our group experiences and the Holy Spirit must be at work.

Redemptive Community: Healing best happens within the context of community and in relationship. A key aspect of our spiritual development is seeing ourselves through the eyes of others, sharing our stories, and ultimately being set free from the secrets and the lies we embrace that enslave our souls.

Mission: God has invited us into a larger story with a great mission. It is a mission that involves setting captives free and healing the broken-hearted (Isaiah 61:1-2). However, we can only join in this mission to the degree that we've let Jesus bind up our wounds and set us free. As a group experiences true redemptive community, other people will be attracted to that group, and through that group to Jesus. We should be alert to inviting others while we maintain (and continue to fill) an "empty chair" in our meetings to remind us of others who need to encounter God and authentic Christian community.

Stages of Group Life

Each healthy small group will move through various stages as it matures. There is no prescribed time frame for moving through these stages because each group is unique.

Birth Stage: This is the time in which group members form relationships and begin to develop community.

Multiply Stage: The group begins the multiplication process. Members pray about their involvement in establishing new groups. The new groups begin the cycle again with the Birth Stage.

Growth Stage: Here the group members begin to care for one another as they learn what it means to apply what they have discovered through Bible study, shared experiences, worship, and prayer.

Develop Stage: The Bible study and shared experiences deepen while the group members develop their gifts and skills. The group explores ways to invite neighbors, friends, and coworkers to meetings.

Subgrouping: If you have more than 12 people at a meeting, Serendipity House recommends dividing into smaller subgroups after the "Breaking the Ice" segment. Ask one person to be the leader of each subgroup, following the "Leader" directions for the session. The Group Leader should bring the subgroups back together for the closing. Subgrouping is also very useful when more openness and intimacy is required. The "Connecting" segment in each session is a great time to divide into smaller groups of four to six people.

Sharing Your Stories

The sessions of *Faith Untamed* are designed to help you share a little of your personal lives with the other people in your group as you grow spiritually. Through your time together, each member of the group is encouraged to move from low risk, less personal sharing to higher risk communication. Real community will not develop apart from increasing intimacy of the group over time.

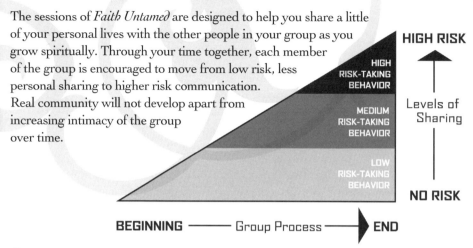

HIGH RISK

HIGH RISK-TAKING BEHAVIOR

MEDIUM RISK-TAKING BEHAVIOR

LOW RISK-TAKING BEHAVIOR

Levels of Sharing

NO RISK

BEGINNING ——— Group Process ——▶ END

Sharing Your Lives

As you share your lives together during this time, it is important to recognize that it is God who has brought each person to this group, gifting the individuals to play a vital role in the group (1 Corinthians 12:1). Each of you was uniquely designed to contribute in your own unique way to building into the lives of the other people in your group. As you get to know one another better, consider the following four areas that will be unique for each person. These areas will help you get a "grip" on how you can better support others and how they can support you.

G – Spiritual Gifts: God has given you unique spiritual gifts (1 Corinthians 12; Romans 12:3-8; Ephesians 4:1-16; etc.).

R – Resources: You have resources that perhaps only you can share, including skill, abilities, possessions, money, and time (Acts 2:44-47; Ecclesiastes 4:9-12, etc.).

I – Individual Experiences: You have past experiences, both good and bad, that God can use to strengthen others (2 Corinthians 1:3-7; Romans 8:28, etc.).

P – Passions: There are things that excite and motivate you. God has given you those desires and passions to use for His purposes (Psalm 37:4,23; Proverbs 3:5-6,13-18; etc.).

To better understand how a group should function and develop in these four areas, consider going through the Serendipity study entitled *Great Beginnings*.

Welcome to Community

GROUP MEETING STRUCTURE

Each of your group meetings will include a four-part agenda.

1. **Breaking the Ice:** This section includes fun, uplifting questions to warm up the group and help group members get to know one another better as they begin the journey of becoming a connected community. These questions prepare the group for meaningful discussion throughout the session.

2. **Discovering the Truth:** The heart of each session is the interactive Bible study time. The goal is for the group to discover biblical truths through open, discovery questions that lead to further investigation. The emphasis in this section is on understanding what the Bible says through interaction within your group.

   To help the group experience a greater sense of community, it is important for everybody to participate in the "Discovering the Truth" and "Embracing the Truth" discussions. Even though people in a group have differing levels of biblical knowledge, it is vital that group members encourage each other to share what they are observing, thinking, and feeling about the Bible passages. Scripture notes are provided at the end of each session to provide additional Bible understanding.

3. **Embracing the Truth:** All study should direct group members to action and life change. This section continues the Bible study time but with an emphasis on leading the group members toward integrating the truths they have discovered into their lives. The questions are very practical and application-focused.

4. **Connecting:** One of the key goals of this study is to lead group members to grow closer to one another as the group develops a sense of community. This section focuses on further application, as well as opportunities for encouraging, supporting, and praying for one another. There are also opportunities to connect with God and to connect with your own heart.

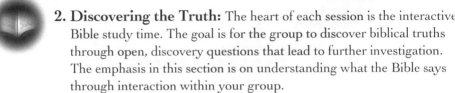

BONUS – Taking it Home: Between each session, there is some homework for group members. This typically includes a question to take to God and a question to take to your heart. These experiences are designed to reinforce the content of the session and help group members deepen their spiritual life and walk with Jesus.

GROUP COVENANT

As you begin this study, it is important that your group covenant together, agreeing to live out important group values. Once these values are agreed upon, your group will be on its way to experiencing true Christian community. It's very important that your group discuss these values—preferably as you begin this study. The first session would be most appropriate.

* **Priority:** While we are in this group, we will give the group meetings priority.

* **Participation:** Everyone is encouraged to participate and no one dominates.

* **Respect:** Everyone is given the right to his or her own opinions, and all questions are encouraged and respected.

* **Confidentiality:** Anything that is said in our meetings is never repeated outside the meeting without permission.

* **Life Change:** We will regularly assess our progress toward applying the "steps" to an amazing marriage. We will complete the "Taking it Home" activities to reinforce what we are learning and better integrate those lessons into our lives.

* **Care and Support:** Permission is given to call upon each other at any time, especially in times of crisis. The group will provide care for every member.

* **Accountability:** We agree to let the members of our group hold us accountable to commitments we make in whatever loving ways we decide upon. Unsolicited advice giving is not permitted.

* **Empty Chair:** Our group will work together to fill the empty chair with an unchurched person or couple.

* **Mission:** We agree as a group to reach out and invite others to join us and to work toward multiplication of our group to form new groups.

* **Ministry:** We will encourage one another to volunteer to serve in a ministry and to support missions work by giving financially and/or personally serving.

I agree to all of the above_____ **date:** _____

ACKNOWLEDGMENTS

We especially want to thank …
- Publisher Ron Keck for his vision
- Writer Ivey Beckman for the passion she brings and her own journey of a faith untamed.
- Darin Clark for art direction and Brian Marschall for cover design
- The editorial team of Bethany McShurley, Jessica Weaver, and Brian Daniel
- Stacey Owens for an eye for detail

About the Authors

MEETING PLANNER

The leader or facilitator of our group is _____ .
The apprentice facilitator for this group is _____ .

We will meet on the following dates and times:

	Date	Day	Time
Session 1	_____	_____	_____
Session 2	_____	_____	_____
Session 3	_____	_____	_____
Session 4	_____	_____	_____
Session 5	_____	_____	_____
Session 6	_____	_____	_____

We will meet at:

Session 1	_____
Session 2	_____
Session 3	_____
Session 4	_____
Session 5	_____
Session 6	_____

Childcare will be arranged by: Refreshments by:

Session 1	_____	_____
Session 2	_____	_____
Session 3	_____	_____
Session 4	_____	_____
Session 5	_____	_____
Session 6	_____	_____

Meeting Planner

GROUP DIRECTORY

Write your name on this page. Pass your books around and ask your group members to fill in their names and contact information in each other's books.

Your Name: _____

Group Directory

Name: _____
Address: _____
City: _____
Zip Code: _____
Home Phone: _____
Mobile Phone: _____
E-mail: _____

Name: _____
Address: _____
City: _____
Zip Code: _____
Home Phone: _____
Mobile Phone: _____
E-mail: _____

Name: _____
Address: _____
City: _____
Zip Code: _____
Home Phone: _____
Mobile Phone: _____
E-mail: _____

Name: _____
Address: _____
City: _____
Zip Code: _____
Home Phone: _____
Mobile Phone: _____
E-mail: _____

Name: _____
Address: _____
City: _____
Zip Code: _____
Home Phone: _____
Mobile Phone: _____
E-mail: _____

Name: _____
Address: _____
City: _____
Zip Code: _____
Home Phone: _____
Mobile Phone: _____
E-mail: _____

Name: _____
Address: _____
City: _____
Zip Code: _____
Home Phone: _____
Mobile Phone: _____
E-mail: _____

Name: _____
Address: _____
City: _____
Zip Code: _____
Home Phone: _____
Mobile Phone: _____
E-mail: _____

Name: _____
Address: _____
City: _____
Zip Code: _____
Home Phone: _____
Mobile Phone: _____
E-mail: _____

Name: _____
Address: _____
City: _____
Zip Code: _____
Home Phone: _____
Mobile Phone: _____
E-mail: _____

Name: _____
Address: _____
City: _____
Zip Code: _____
Home Phone: _____
Mobile Phone: _____
E-mail: _____

Name: _____
Address: _____
City: _____
Zip Code: _____
Home Phone: _____
Mobile Phone: _____
E-mail: _____